I Say Yes to Life:
The Affirmation Project

By: David W. Jones

Dear Peggy,

    May this book inspire you to love yourself more, say YES to Life, and be grateful always. Thank you for being such a wonderful friend to my Teddy.

All my love,

I Say Yes to Life: The Affirmation Project

ISBN 978-1-0879-8811-5

For Jill.

Thank you for sharing your beautiful light in the world and in my life. I will think of you every time I see the color purple. Thank you for being an important part of this book; I treasure every moment we spent together. You truly lived a life of service to your family, your church, your students and your community. You are missed.

I love you!

Table of Contents

Foreword 2

By Hunter Flournoy

Author's Introduction 4

Section I: The Courage to Heal 9

1. I am looking at my life and my choices without judgment.
2. I choose to ask for help.
3. I am not alone.
4. We heal in community.
5. I am safe.
6. It's okay to be anxious.
7. This too shall pass.
8. I choose to be optimistic.
9. Change can be a good thing.
10. Not all recovery looks the same.

Section II: Self Discovery 31

1. I am grateful.
2. I am good enough.
3. I am lovable.
4. I am not broken.
5. I am creative.
6. I am unique.
7. I am strong.
8. I am a survivor.
9. I am resilient.
10. I am grateful to be alive.

Section III: Stretching My Wings 53

1. Gratitude is a gateway to freedom.
2. I create my own spirituality.
3. I choose to be gentle with my body.
4. I relax my grip.
5. I take my foot off the gas.
6. I give up my image of perfection.
7. I forgive myself.
8. I forgive myself for not being able to forgive.
9. I will keep showing up. I will not give up.
10. My story has value.
11. I can change my story.
12. Every choice I make creates the masterpiece that is my life.

Section IV: Trusting Myself to Fly 79

1.   Gratitude is my foundation.
2.   I trust the process of healing my life.
3.   I trust myself to meet the unknown.
4.   Life speaks to me. I listen.
5.   I trust my intuition.
6.   I love and accept my body.
7.   I love myself.
8.   I am a gift to this world.
9.   I shine.
10. The light of God shines through me.

Section V: I am Free...101

1.   Love is the answer.
2.   I let it go.
3.   I can breathe.
4.   My breath connects me to the present moment.
5.   My center is a still pond.
6.   I am content.
7.   I am at Peace.

Afterword: We are artists. Our lives are our art.................117

Resources: Prayer and Meditation 121

1.   My Third Step Prayer
2.   Meditation: This too shall Pass.
3.   Meditation: On Gratitude.
4.   Meditation: On Self-Forgiveness.
5.   Meditation: For Self-Love.
6.   Meditation: My Center is a Still Pond.

Photo Credits 132

Foreword

In thirty years of recovery and twenty-eight years of leading retreats and working in homeless shelters, mental health centers, inpatient treatment, and private practice, I have met few who shine as brightly as David Jones. His endurance, creativity, generosity, and spiritual depth are extraordinary.

He brought the same qualities to his addiction, of course, for what is addiction if not a fiercely determined response to the suffering of our lives? The ferocity of his suffering was visible in the hard light gleaming from his eyes when I first met him. Terrible loss, abuse, and a family history of addiction had driven him into a desperate and chaotic search for relief, security, belonging, and control for many years. There was something else in his eyes, though: a bright coal of self-love and tremendous courage glowed brightly under the ashes.

I was there as David realized his strength and identified the ways that power had been misdirected by trauma and addiction. I watched as he questioned the stories that reinforced those patterns. I cheered as he began to recognize and receive the love and support that waited for him. I stepped back in wonder as David performed a miracle; he realized that he had the power to make a different choice. He began saying yes to his own life one day at a time.

One of the most remarkable things about David's journey is his mastery of that most difficult art: creating a recovery path that is uniquely his while also drawing upon the enormous wisdom, support, and clear-eyed feedback of his trusted recovery team and the twelve-step tradition. Too often, addicts in early recovery are taught to mistrust their inner compass instead of cultivating their relationship with the voice of truth inside them. Too often, they are shamed for their addiction instead of understanding the real wisdom and deep unmet needs behind their self-destructive behavior. David did the hard work of learning to discern the voice of his heart from the voice of his addiction and discovered the extraordinary courage to follow it. He gleaned the essential truths from every spiritual tradition he encountered, integrated them into a cohesive and potent spiritual discipline, and leaned into the wealth of loving support and guidance around him. He created LGBTQ recovery groups, founded an intentional recovery community, and began sharing his experience, strength, and hope with countless students in his trauma-informed yoga classes in communities, churches, and treatment centers. Every time he shared his experience, his yearning to share it grew, and he began creating this book.

Over the last twenty years, I have had the joy and honor of bearing witness to David's miracle. With this book in your hands, you have the same opportunity. You will walk beside him as he makes the life-changing discovery that none of us are alone or can recover alone; we need each other like we need the air we breathe. You will discover with him what it truly means to love oneself and to open oneself to the grace of one's life. You will realize with him the power to re-direct your thoughts, your love, and your strength towards lifting yourself up, reaching out, and cultivating – one choice at a time – a life of sobriety, self-care, and passionate service.

These pages hold yet another gift for you, one that David has devoted his whole life to cultivating. He has mastered the power of affirmation. Many think of affirmation as an effort to convince oneself of something that isn't true. Other people believe that affirmations are like magic charms to conjure a new reality into being. David's life and work demonstrate the true power of affirmations: they affirm what is deepest and truest in our own experience, nourishing those truths and bringing them into our activities and relationships, creating lives that reflect our most passionately held values and dreams.

What is deeply and completely true in your own heart? How do those truths want to be lived out in your life? What hidden reservoirs of strength lie hidden within you? How can you cultivate the patient self-love to answer all these questions? I have seen David Jones live his way into the answers. I have watched the self-love which powers his recovery overflow into the lives of everyone he encounters, inspiring and transforming us all with a vision of what our lives can be and the love that waits to embrace us. I am excited for you to discover your truth and affirm that truth with your whole life.

Congratulations on finding this book. May the greatness within us become the lives we share.

Hunter Flournoy, MFA, MS, LPC

Introduction to The Power of Affirmation

I'd like to invite you on a journey to a new way of thinking and being in your life through the power of affirmation. This journey has the power to change our perceptions of ourselves, our world, our self-talk, our emotions, and our attitudes. It will affirm our strengths, resilience, abilities, and worthiness of being loved. We will move from negativity to positivity, from putting ourselves down to lifting ourselves up. Together, we will explore how I have overcome challenges, changed belief systems, and turned around my self-hatred – and how you can do the same in your own life. Every affirmation will take you one more step to greater self-love.

My History

To help you better understand the difference affirmations have made in my life, I should tell you where I started. I didn't think I would make it this far. I experienced the trauma of sexual abuse and abandonment as a child and a teenager, growing up in a household with two alcoholic parents. When I was ten, my mother had an aneurysm and spent the remaining twenty-three years of her life in a nursing home. The course of my life changed in dramatic ways, landing me in a British boarding school in Australia for five years and bringing an emotionally abusive stepmother into my life.

In response, I cultivated any addiction that would make me feel better, different, or numb, and developed self-harm behaviors like cutting and overworking myself to injury or exhaustion. Codependency almost killed me many times as I went from one dangerous relationship to another, trying to take care of myself by taking care of others. I had no idea how to care for myself or even be alone. As a result, I had a lot of pain to medicate, and my physical scars tell a story of pain, self-hatred, and anger turned inward. I have been close to death many times, including twice by my own hands.

My recovery journey began over thirty years ago. I did my best to work recovery the way other people told me to in the twelve-step rooms. For some people, the "rules and regulations" of twelve-step recovery are just what they need; for me, the most valuable part of the program was the invitation to "take what you need and leave the rest." As a trauma survivor, I didn't have a voice and didn't feel as if I had any power. To heal, I needed to be the author of my recovery and discover that power. "To Thine Own Self be True" is engraved on every twelve-step medallion. These words have guided my life.

Once I discovered the strength of my voice and my power to choose, I was able to open myself up to guidance in my recovery; I recognized that my best thinking had gotten me where I was in my addiction. Guidance takes many forms and can be different for every person. My connection with God, spiritual practices, and people further ahead of me in recovery helped me the most.

In the fall of 2002, after two years of IV drug and crack cocaine use, I found myself in middle Tennessee at The Recovery Ranch, where I stayed for three and a half months. My time at the Ranch was the beginning of my deeper dive into healing and recovery because it was there that I discovered the teachings and practices that would mold the next two decades of my life and help me create and thrive in a life that I love and enjoy. I asked for help and guidance, and God, in His grace, led me to co-create the community of Laughing Winds, a support system of sober people trying to live authentic lives. I began working on a deeper level to make my recovery path my own, incorporating AA, Toltec Wisdom, and Yoga into my life. All these working together made me into the sober, solid man I am today.

The Pillars of my Recovery

Looking back now, I recognize six gifts that became the pillars of my recovery program.

The first two came from my parents. My Dad blessed me with his optimism, strength, and shining spirit; from him, I learned to believe in the power of positive thinking. One of my father's gifts was his ever-present and infectious optimism. He always had a twinkle in his eye and never met a stranger. Even though it sometimes led to him being taken advantage of, he always saw the best in everyone. I learned early on that every cloud has a silver lining; in my experience, it truly has. I attribute my stamina and strength to my father. He lived to be 94 and never lost his cheerful outlook on life. Even though he was always away working when I was a child, he never abandoned me as an adult. He bailed me out of every jam I got into financially and legally. He was also a writer; travelogs mostly, but he shared them with family and friends far and wide as he traveled the world with my stepmother. My father was a successful businessman, which provided me with an affluent life and the best medical care. My life journey of sixty years has been challenging, and my life expectancy at times uncertain, but thanks in large part to my father, my glass has been half full instead of half empty.

My mother gave me her gifts of artistry, spirituality, and an appreciation for the finer things in life. I was always well dressed and grew up in a beautiful home. She taught me about refinement, beauty, and grace. She had impeccable style and perhaps gave me her expensive taste. I don't think we missed a Sunday at church. She had sewed a needlepoint altar kneeling cushion, which speaks to her devotion to her faith. While my Dad's church was on his boat, my mother was the one who shaped my early belief in God. She was also an artist. There was often an easel on the dining room table. I can still smell the oils she used to paint. She often had trouble finishing a piece, as she was a perfectionist. I have a still life she painted of her prayer book and bible with a glass of sherry and her wedding ring. I call it her self-portrait.

I believe my parents gave me the best of themselves. While they gave me their genes for addiction, they also gave me intelligence, artistry, creativity, beauty, strength, stamina, a big smile, and a shining spirit. My sister Tish also needs mentioning as she was my safe haven when we were kids. Although she was only six years older, she became my 'mother' when our mother became ill. She has never abandoned me and supported me with unconditional love, and I wouldn't be here without her. If I understand anything about safety and family in my life now, it is because Tish was my safety for so long and taught me the importance of real family and unconditional love.

The other three gifts came much later. The next gift was the teachings of my mentor Hunter Flournoy, whom I still work with today. His guidance, support, and love created the foundation of my growth and healing. He has been a constant shining light of love and inspiration and a huge part of writing this book. He taught me that compassion is a superpower and showed me how to create relationships with my inner child and the parts of me that I hated, which needed my love the most. He has witnessed my growth through many life-changing challenges in our years together. He helped me create a program of recovery that worked for me. He taught me how to love myself and stand in my power. He has brought out the best in me and showed me how to be the teacher I am.

The next gift was The Toltec Path, which began with the book "The Four Agreements" by Don Miguel Ruiz and included an apprenticeship, mystery school, working with extraordinary teachers, and many trips to the pyramid city of Teotihuacan in Mexico. These teachings taught me that I could change the story of my life. I learned to see my pain and the strategies I used to medicate it as gifts in my growing process. I learned how to create my spirituality, and I came to know God in a much deeper way. I learned how to use my intention to tap into Source and create a new life, letting go of the past and living in the now, working with the flow of life in ways I never thought possible. I learned how to look at myself and my choices through the eyes of love instead of fear.

The final gift was a Toltec teacher named Barbara Simon, my first yoga teacher. Yoga felt good for my out-of-shape body and helped calm my anxiety and ease my anger and depression. I stuck with it and soon began teaching at The Ranch, a beginner teaching beginners. Yoga has become a life path and has helped me on many levels. I credit it with saving my life, as it got me through post-cancer depression. Teaching yoga has always given me something to show up and be sober for when I don't want to get out of bed. Yoga gives me physical, mental, and spiritual health and the stamina to keep showing up, doing the work, and moving forward in my life. One of the niyamas of yoga is ishvarapranidhana, which translates as "trustful surrender to God," or giving self and life over to a higher purpose. With a foundation of gratitude, I practice radical self-love (loving myself no matter what) daily, and I try to be of service with my yoga ministry.

Using these gifts and drawing upon the support and wisdom of many teachers and God, I have healed my sadness and built a strong foundation of gratitude and self-love. These are also the gifts I share now as a healer and teacher. After trying not to feel for the first forty years of my life, I feel things deeply now. I no longer carry the cloud of sadness that hung over me for the first forty years of my life. There is still work to do, but the work I have already done has me thriving, and the sunlight of my spirit shines. Finally, I created a relationship that wasn't based on codependency; God has gifted me with the most wonderful man in my partner Teddy Jones to walk beside me. He provides a safe haven for me to continue to heal. I hope to spend the rest of my life holding his hand.

My Journey with These Memes

These affirmation memes tell how I have overcome codependency, addictions, and self-harm behaviors and healed much of the underlying trauma. They affirm my courage and resilience, self-love and gratitude, healing and trust in the process, and faith in God. Some of them are guides to create change or affirm my inherent value. All of them have come out of my life experience on my path of recovery.

This book of affirmation memes came about through my work as a trauma-sensitive yoga teacher at the Ranch Recovery Center and Milestones at Onsite, residential mental health and trauma treatment centers in Middle Tennessee. I have put the affirmations in the form of memes, using many of my photographs. In each affirmation meme, I have shared parts of my story, how the affirmation came out of my life experience, and how I have met some of the challenges on the way. I have worked at Milestones for the last seven years, using these affirmations to share my trauma and addiction recovery with their clients. I have published these affirmations on Facebook and Instagram over the past three years, even though some are very personal, and I felt pretty vulnerable putting them out in the world. Every step has grown me.

Writing and sharing my story has been empowering, freeing, and healing. I have been amazed at the positive feedback I have received, especially on the edgier ones. I want to be as transparent as possible. I will continue to create affirmation memes because there is so much to affirm. There are many ways to teach about love, gratitude, change, growth, compassion, and forgiveness and affirm our power, strength, and courage. I hope these images and words will inspire you to show up, keep going, create a life you love, and let your light shine bright, even with all your self-doubt and imperfections. After all, it's our imperfections that make us beautiful.

Your Journey with These Memes

Affirmations help me put my energy and attention on the solution and not the problem. What we focus our energy on grows. Each of these 51 affirmations focuses on something I have struggled with in my journey of healing and recovery. We practice saying an affirmation until we believe what we are affirming. Affirmations have the power to change our brain chemistry. We can use them to train ourselves and our minds to think more positively. We can strengthen our will, our faith in God, and the power of our healing process. Affirmations teach us to look for the good in people and in life. All these affirmations together are windows into my soul. They affirm as a whole that I say YES to life.

I wrote the affirmations in the first person, so the reader can say them as written and 'own' them with all their energy and intent. After telling you how the affirmation has worked for me or come to be in my life, I ask you to see how it resonates with you, what it brings up, and how you might use it. At times in my life, I have put affirmations on post-it notes on my dash, bathroom mirror, or inside a kitchen cabinet as reminders to say the affirmation, often like a mantra.

I hope this book will inspire you to create and work with your affirmations. They have been one of the tools in my mental health toolkit for a while now. I enjoyed creating and pulling them together, and I am proud of my work creating this book. I couldn't have made it without an excellent support team. I hope you know who you are and how grateful I am for your support. It was a blessed day when I learned to ask for help, but it was a long time coming. I will keep showing up and doing my best to be a loving human who practices compassion. As it says at the end of The Big Book of AA, "More will be revealed." Enjoy your life journey and be curious. Amazing and miraculous things happen, but we are often too self-absorbed to notice. I invite you to join me in slowing down, taking a nourishing breath, and affirming with me, "I say yes to life."

All my love,
David

Section I : The Courage to Heal

I am looking at my life and my choices without judgment.

This is always the first affirmation on my list when I teach our affirmation classes. I was so full of judgment when I found myself in drug and alcohol treatment 20 years ago. I had so much judgment about my addiction and mental health issues. This is probably why I found the path of yoga incredibly healing, with its focus on love, compassion, and non-judgment. I learned to look at my choices and see what works and what doesn't without judgment. If I don't like the results of my choice, I can modify it or make another choice moving forward. I don't have to judge myself. I just choose again.

When I began loving myself more and judging myself less, I found one day, to my surprise, that I didn't hate myself anymore. When my students asked how I got there, I realized there was no quick, easy answer. It took the constant practice of radical self-love – loving myself no matter what. It took lots of self-care, self-forgiveness, compassion, trusting myself, and trusting the healing process. It took putting one foot in front of the other, moving forward, and not giving up. Overcoming my self-hatred has been one of the greatest gifts of yoga and recovery – one that took a lot of hard work.

We all judge ourselves too often, and judgment can mean punishment. Punishment doesn't do any good either; it just leads to more judgment. I invite you to close your eyes, take a breath with me, and let go of self-doubting, self-judging, and self-punishing for a moment. Consider the possibility that everyone is so self-absorbed that they are not judging us nearly as much as we think! Remember that judging – especially judging ourselves – isn't going to help anything: practice patience, compassion, and forgiveness with yourself. Give yourself a break, trust that you have been doing your best all along, and you are where you are supposed to be in your life. Consider the possibility that you are worthy, loveable, and good enough. I invite you to affirm with me, "I am looking at my life and my choices without judgment."

I choose to ask for help.

I had a breakthrough moment in treatment twenty years ago. Until that moment, I had spent my entire life making huge messes over and over again, repeating the same mistakes and leaving my family to clean them up and bail me out. I tried to figure everything out on my own, often by doing the exact same things and expecting different results.

One day in group therapy, a miracle happened. I was doing my usual – trying to figure it all out, trying to fix myself on my own, feeling frustrated and stuck. Suddenly, I saw myself, and I realized what I was doing. A new possibility occurred to me. I realized I could ask for help.

This realization might seem simple, but it had never occurred to me! I saw my whole life with new eyes. I began to practice asking for help when I needed it instead of waiting for the mess! I made fewer messes, and when I did make one, it was smaller. I became more humble and teachable as I recognized and accepted my limitations. In the past, I felt ashamed of my limitations; now, I see them as opportunities for grace. Asking for help takes an enormous weight off my shoulders! I have discovered that I don't have to do it all alone. This simple insight has genuinely become the foundation of my whole recovery.

Even after this realization, addiction brought me to my knees many times. Something had changed, however: every time I felt powerless, ashamed, and afraid, I remembered that I could ask for help, and when I did, I experienced God's helping grace. I have been held, guided, and watched over at every turn.

Today I am aware of my limitations, including living with mental health issues, various physical injuries, and managing chronic pain. It has taken many years of just showing up one day at a time, practicing yoga, and working on recovery to learn how to love myself and ask for help. I have a solid support team, making it easy to reach out when needed. Everyone on my team is a manifestation of God working in my life.

Do you know your limitations? Do you ask for help easily? Do you judge yourself if you can't? Are there some places in your life where you could use some help or support? I invite you to think about this affirmation and ask yourself how it might work in your life. There is never any shame in asking for help. I know how hard it can be to pick up the phone when you are hurting, lonely, sad, and full of self-doubt. The challenge is even more significant if you are a lifeline for others, but I promise you, it gets easier. It is so much easier for me than it used to be. Whatever you need help with, reach out and join me in affirming, "I choose to ask for help."

When I finally got to treatment, I was mentally, physically, and spiritually in rough shape. I found others there who had suffered some of the same life challenges as me and who were experiencing the same consequences of addiction. In the end stages of active addiction, I felt desperate, isolated, ashamed, and alone. It wasn't until I got sober in the rooms of AA that I felt safe enough to share stories of my experience, strength, and hope. At last, I found commonality with others around our common addiction problem. I can always reach out to someone in the program when I need support or go to a meeting.

My yoga community helps me feel less alone as well. Teaching trauma-sensitive yoga, I get to be part of another's healing journey for a brief time, sharing my trauma recovery and the power of yoga to help the healing process. It feels like sacred work. I have worked with some of the same students in my church yoga communities for years, and I always receive more than I give. Whenever I go to a yoga class as a teacher or student, I am enveloped in the community and joined together with others by our shared love of yoga.

I also believe we are watched over and loved more than we could ever know: by God, by angels, by our ancestors, and by loved ones who have passed. If we knew that in the deepest well of our being, I think we would have so much less fear, sadness, and despair. Our loved ones who have left us are always with us and can help support us if we ask.

Do you enjoy your own company? Do you feel lonely often? How is your connection with Spirit or God? Do you have difficulty finding community? There are all kinds of support and services on the internet, ways to find people, make connections, and even go to a meeting without leaving the safety of your home. If you are hurting, feeling overwhelmed, or lonely, take a risk and reach out to someone. I have found that it is usually a gift to the one who answers your call. Take a moment and find comfort in the love of all the people who support you in your life. How might they help you even more? I invite you to reach out and connect with someone and affirm with me, "I am not alone."

We heal in community.

I co-created an intentional community called "Laughing Winds" nearly twenty years ago in Nunnelly, Tennessee. It was a beautiful sanctuary on the Piney River where people could retreat and rediscover their authentic selves. Living in community taught me a lot about communication, connection, codependency, and boundaries. I learned much about asking for help during those years in community as I navigated cancer and my father's death. We created a family of choice out of an island of misfit toys, a powerful expression of friendship, and our shared commitment to freedom from addiction, self-doubt, and the pressures we put ourselves through. I experienced so much growth and healing over the many years I lived in the community of Laughing Winds.

Other communities also contributed to my healing. In AA and twelve-step recovery meetings, I found instant community. This kind of community is one of the most significant gifts of the program; we share our stories and find commonality and connection with each other around our common addiction problem. It is healing to be listened to and heard in a safe environment.

I also love my yoga community and the people I reach through my yoga ministry at treatment centers and various church groups. These circles of support have held me in a container of love and given me purpose when I've been depressed. I have facilitated healing for many, but I always feel I receive more than I give.

I have also spent years in the gay community. I've participated in marches and pride parades, been active in the arts, and volunteered at gay community centers. I've created gay 12-step groups and taught yoga at spiritual conferences for gay men. I am so grateful to have witnessed all we have achieved as a community in my lifetime.

What circles of community give you the feeling of belonging? Do you need more community in your life? Sometimes in the absence of community, we have to create it ourselves; think about what you can do to find or create new community in your life. How can you deepen your connections with the communities you already enjoy? Reach out to the people in your life. Share your stories. Be vulnerable, and take the risk of being more authentic. Seek opportunities to be of service in your communities. Recognize and appreciate the communities you already love. Open yourself up to the healing gifts of being in community, acknowledge them with gratitude, and affirm with me, "We heal in community."

Safety means different things to different people. Having lots of money in the bank makes some of us feel safe. Some of us think that guns will keep us safe. We wear seat belts in cars and planes to keep us safe. We build walls and have security systems to keep us safe.

For trauma survivors, safety is a more internal thing. For many years, I didn't feel safe in my own body. My body's animal urges and chemical dependencies betrayed me, and I became powerless over sex, drugs, and anything that would numb my feelings and calm my anxiety. Like many trauma survivors, I suffered from hypervigilance, generalized anxiety, and an ever-present alertness that keeps my nervous system in high arousal. We survivors are sensitive, perceptive, and often empathic, and we can go into fight, flight, freeze, or collapse at the slightest trigger. As a result, I felt unsafe even when it was irrational to do so.

Creating safety in my life took time and dedication, and I had to do that before I could heal my deeper core wounds. God gifted me with a living, breathing teddy bear in my partner Teddy Jones to hold me in a container of unconditional love while I healed. His love and affection have soothed away my tears and fears. Long-term therapy and many healing workshops facilitated work with my inner child, which led to my younger self finally trusting me to take care of him. I surrounded myself with sober people choosing to live authentically, and I let the land and Nature soothe my rough edges like a balm.

What makes you feel safe? Who are the people who are lifelines for you? A lifeline for me is someone I call when I need comforting, who will give me honest feedback when I need help making difficult decisions. Think about who you trust and what supports you in your life. When we feel safe, we relax into trust and can start the process of healing. I invite you to close your eyes, soften your jaw, relax your shoulders, take a few deep breaths, and as you exhale, affirm with me, "I am safe."

It's okay to be anxious.

I have been anxious my whole life. My close friends know this about me, and it has given us a laugh when I would wring my hands over the idea that unexpected visitors would show up in our community and require feeding. There was always enough food to go around, so my worry was for nothing.

My anxiety and activated nervous system came from not feeling safe as a child and as a teenager in boarding school. Today, anxiety shows up in many other ways: rushing around when it is not necessary, driving too fast, not breathing deeply, having a short attention span, and not being able to be still. Plenty is going on right now to make me feel unsafe! All I have to do is read or watch the news and think about all the divisions in our country, and I get anxious.

It is good that I have chosen the life path of a yogi, as yoga teaches me the skills to manage my anxiety, such as asana (movement), pranayama (breathing), and meditation, to name a few. The biggest anxiety-management skill, though, is simply to practice non-judgment. I accept that I am anxious by nature, and there is plenty to feel anxious about, so I choose (to the best of my ability) not to judge it. I accept that this anxiety might not ever change. Whether I am anxious or feeling peaceful, I love myself today, and even with my ever-present anxiety, I am more at peace now than ever.

At the same time, it might change! I thought the same thing about many other challenges that **have** changed with a bit of work and faith on my part. I know God watches over me, and I trust in the safety of His grace. I know I will be okay. I have put myself in some perilous situations in my life; but I have always been guided, protected, watched over, and given many second chances.

Do you live with anxiety? Do you judge it? How does it affect your life? The bottom line is that we all experience much more stress than we are used to, with so many unknowns. Fear and anxiety are normal responses, and we must learn to care for ourselves and do things that reduce stress. Mindful, slow breathing can help, so can a hot bath or shower, or walking in Nature. The important thing is that we don't judge our anxiety and understand that everyone lives with some degree of it. I invite you to join me in affirming: "It's okay to be anxious."

When I was in the valleys of physical illness, addiction, and depression, it seemed as if I would never get out. When recovering from cancer, I never thought I would get my energy back.

I am so thankful I was wrong; Life always came in to support me through friends, family, nature, and faith. I have found that the things I am most afraid of do not usually turn out to be as scary or awful as I project and anticipate. I have found that times of suffering do pass. Hopefully, the pain from the oral surgery I had today will be gone in a week.

On a larger scale, the collective stress of the challenges we are living through with the Covid pandemic and the political stress we live under seems like more than I can bear. I don't see the way forward for our nation and global community. Still, I know that Humanity has survived many global challenges; even extinctions have come and gone, and this planet and we humans have survived.

I still believe that most people want connection. Even in these challenging times, people often return a smile or a wave. These challenges will change us and the way we do some things, and those changes won't be all bad. Who knows what is on the other side of it all? It will pass, though, and we will be stronger for it. Or not? Only time will tell.

Maybe there is a silver lining to the pandemic. Perhaps it is waking us up to truths we didn't want to see. What are you ready to move past in your life? What do you want to stop worrying about? Are you dealing with a crisis? More often than not, we get well after being sick. Grief eventually softens as we remember our loved ones who have passed. Even wars finally pass. Our government changes every two years. Many things that cause us suffering today won't matter in a year. We will have moved on. Change is the only constant in the Universe. I invite you to consider those things you are ready to move past, let go of, and stop worrying about. Life is too short to spend stressed out in fear and anxiety. Please acknowledge and affirm with me that, "This too shall pass."

I choose to be optimistic.

One of the greatest gifts my father gave me was his optimism; he always said every cloud has a silver lining. I believe in positive thinking, and I think happiness is a choice. I believe our thoughts create our choices, and our choices create our reality. I believe the only thing we have control over is our attitude.

I teach a lot about living with an attitude of gratitude, as it is the foundation of my life. Being optimistic is not always easy, but an upbeat attitude is incredibly helpful when we start on the road to recovery or healing from any trauma. I carried a cloud of sadness over my head most of my life, but I am grateful that I haven't seen that cloud for many years, thanks to the sunshine of my loving and decades of committed practice.

We need affirmations in times of challenge. I choose to see the glass as half-full most of the time, but it's the opposite some days. Even on those days, I work hard to make sure my choices don't come from a place of fear. I remind myself that I have gotten through everything I have ever been afraid of. I remember that most things are never as bad as I imagined. I am now on the other side of so many things I was afraid of in the past.

Could you choose to be more optimistic in your life? Do you see your glass as half-full or half-empty? From my experience, choosing to have an optimistic attitude changes everything for the better. What we focus on and give our energy to grows. Look for the good in every situation. I invite you to choose to believe in the benevolence of the Universe and trust that there is enough for everyone. Choose to see life through the eyes of love rather than fear. Take a breath and open your heart in gratitude and affirm with me, "I choose to be optimistic."

Change can be a good thing.

I used to be afraid of change. It's not hard to track that back to childhood when dramatic changes occurred that were out of my control and caused me suffering and pain. I used to see life from a worm's eye view; now, I can see the bigger picture and understand why some things had to happen to become the man I am, whom I love today.

Now, instead of being afraid of change, I seek it out and embrace it. Just because change has been difficult in the past doesn't mean change is always going to be hard. I trust in God, the benevolence of the Universe, and my ability to respond to life's challenges. Most of the time, things I have been afraid of have not turned out to be as bad as my thoughts imagined.

From my point of view, we can create change, embrace it, and go with the flow of Life, or we can resist it, be a victim of it, and suffer. In this photo, you will see a picture of total change and transformation. I trust that change is good and can take me to places I never imagined. I am no longer a caterpillar; I have transformed into something altogether different and exceptional.

What things can you change in your life that might bring you more happiness and peace? Do you have some beliefs that make you suffer? Are you in a relationship that is draining your energy? Do you say yes when you mean no? We only have to start with some small positive, manageable things, like moving a few things in our living space or changing how we do a menial task, or perhaps how we drive home from work. Tiny changes can lead to bigger changes, and soon we will be like the caterpillar, turning into something different. I challenge you to believe in the power of positive thinking and affirm with me, "Change can be a good thing."

Not all recovery looks the same.

It took me a long time to come to this affirmation, but I think it is helpful to hear it early on. My definition of addiction is the experience we have when something becomes more powerful than our ability to control or stop it, usually with destructive and harmful consequences. I know addiction inside and out. I have used sex, work, alcohol, self-harm, and IV drugs to medicate the intense emotional pain I was feeling for most of my life. I have casually put myself in dangerous and high-risk situations to satisfy my addiction to anxiety and the adrenaline of an over-activated nervous system. I have lived addiction, and I have survived experiences I shouldn't have survived.

I was introduced to yoga twenty years ago at The Recovery Ranch when I committed to stop using alcohol and drugs. Yoga became an essential part of my recovery, but it also became my new addiction. I was addicted to the adrenaline rush and endorphins I get from an active yoga class. Yoga satisfied my addiction to intensity, but there were consequences in the form of injuries. I was powerless over pushing my body hard every time. Still, even with injuries, yoga was an addiction upgrade from alcohol and drugs.

Harm reduction is the guiding principle of my recovery. For some addictions, the only way to reduce harm is simply to stop. For other addictions like my addiction to self-harm – intense yoga practice, for example – I started with the goal of weaning off rather than abruptly stopping a behavior. I switched to other less harmful ways to medicate my anxiety and emotional pain. My relationship with yoga, for example, was out of balance and had to change. I shifted my focus to healing my body with restorative yoga, pranayama, and meditation.

I have not always done as I have been advised, but I have created a program of recovery that works for me. I am sober, and my life is stable and balanced. I have found that sometimes addiction is more about our relationship to the thing or behavior in question. We can be addicted to something that is an upgrade from a more harmful predecessor. I invite you to look at your relationships with things that throw you and your life out of balance. Find healthy things to do that make you feel good and don't have negative consequences. If you are powerless over what you are doing and there are negative consequences, you might want to stop it. I invite you to keep moving forward into your healing and recovery, one step, one breath at a time. Find what works for you. I believe intention is a powerful thing. When we set our intention to heal and recover, Life supports us in so many ways. Join me in affirming, "Not all recovery looks the same."

Section II : Self Discovery

I am grateful for so much. I wrote this affirmation eight weeks into recovery
from a successful back and prostate surgery. I was relieved of the pain I had
been living with for so long! To be pain-free after surgery was indeed a miracle.
I felt free in a way I hadn't felt in a long time. Years of bending over my students,
giving them adjustments, and pushing my body had finally caught up with me,
and I had been suffering from back issues for years before I had the surgery. I
had waited until I could no longer bend over, drive, or do my job.

I am grateful for all the little miracles that made this big miracle possible. I am
grateful for modern medicine and a great surgeon. I am grateful for the power
of prayer. I am grateful for community. I am grateful for my partner Teddy who
never left my side and cared for my every need. I am grateful for all the people
who wished me well, prayed for me, cooked me food, and sent flowers. I am
grateful for this body that heals quickly. I am grateful to be back at work, doing
work I love that nourishes my spirit. I am grateful to have just had a milestone
birthday. I am grateful for friends who are lifelines. I am grateful to my teachers
and therapists. I am grateful for yoga and its continued healing of my body,
mind, and spirit. I am grateful for my recovery. I am grateful for my family
of origin and my family of choice. I am grateful for the little luxuries I didn't

recognize until now. I am grateful for my beautiful home. I am grateful to be alive. I am grateful for healing. I am grateful for God's love and grace, and I am grateful for all of you, my friends.

What are you grateful for? Practicing gratitude will transform your life because it did mine. It can move you from looking at your life from a place of lack, unworthiness, or victimization into a place of appreciation and connection. To begin with, start your day by naming a few things that you are grateful for. Do it before bed as well. Or perhaps when you look at your phone, all the same digits line up. Whenever you see something out in the world that lifts you or opens your heart, acknowledge that something bigger than you is at work in your life. This practice helped turn around my depression after my chemotherapy. Today gratitude is a way of life for me. There is always something to be grateful for, from clean drinkable water from the tap to hot showers to grocery stores. I hope you will take time to name the things you feel grateful for and affirm with me, "I am grateful."

I am good enough.

I think one of the earliest lies we come to believe is that we aren't good enough. We learn that there is some measure of good, bad, better, and best. Some of us even believe that we need to be perfect to be loved. Often our parents and teachers had high expectations and even punished us if we didn't measure up. I spent most of my life raising the bar every time I met it.

I spent five years in a British boarding school in Australia, so I know a lot about the pressure to be the best little boy in the world. I was only an average student, so I missed the rewards of praise from my parents. I learned to feel not good enough, and as a result, I have struggled with perfectionism all of my life. I also carried a lot of shame and wounding around sexual trauma. I didn't have any self-esteem and thought I wasn't very exciting. As a child, I experienced my family looking perfect on the outside but feeling far from perfect on the inside. I learned early that a smile and a laugh cover up a lot of pain.

I know today that I am good enough without having to do or be anything other than who I am. I have been working on this affirmation for a long time; it was one of the first and most important. I have spent years confronting the lie that I am not good enough and affirming my worth. It took patience and lots of compassion to learn to love myself. It also took others modeling it for me. Of course, that doesn't stop me from judging myself sometimes when I don't meet my expectations, and my expectations are still high. I know now, however, that judgment is not helpful.

Do you judge yourself for not being good enough? Are you tired of it? I invite you to put this affirmation on a post-it note where you can often see it in a dish cabinet, on a mirror, or on your car dash. Say this affirmation like a mantra, a prayer, a reminder of a more profound truth. Judgment is like a weed rooted deep in the garden of our soul, but this kind of weed only grows in darkness. Shine your daily love and compassion on it, and it will wither.

We are loved so much more than we could ever know, and we are surrounded with so much grace. I invite you to take a breath with me, let go of your perfectionism for a moment and affirm, "I am good enough."

I am lovable.

For so many reasons, I didn't feel wanted when I was a child.

My mother was 42 when she became pregnant with me, and the family used to say that she wasn't that excited about it. My parents were both alcoholics, and as far back as I can remember, they argued and fought a lot, and I blamed myself. My mother had an aneurysm when I was ten and lived for twenty-three years in a nursing home until she died; in any way that mattered, I lost her. My stepmother appeared soon after my mother got sick, and she and my father tried to reclaim their romantic fantasy from when they met in the war. I felt unwanted by her as if I was in the way of her having my father solely for herself; the last thing they seemed to want was to have a sensitive, needy, ten-year-old child along for the ride. I was the lost child in our family system. The trauma of 'losing' my mother, living with an abusive stepmother, and sexual abuse, made me hate myself. I developed self-harm behaviors. I tried my best not to feel, using anything I could to self-medicate. I didn't feel lovable.

I've made great strides in turning that self-hated around in the last fifteen years of sobriety and hard work. I learned how to ask for help, and I learned to trust God and Life. I stopped using things like drugs and alcohol to harm myself and turned around my self-destructive lifestyle. With help, I learned how to help my inner child feel safe and trust the healing process. There have been many people along the way who modeled self-love and helped me love myself. Sacred places have helped me, such as Teotihuacan, an ancient pyramid city in Mexico. I have visited there over twenty times and drank deeply of the love and healing energy there.

Do you feel unlovable? Do you withhold love from yourself? Are you constantly judging yourself or comparing yourself to others? Have compassion for where you are. If you are struggling with self-hatred, know that you can learn to love and trust yourself. We are loved so much more than we could ever comprehend. Begin to look for the people in your life who model self-love. Self-love takes time. Building trust takes time, especially after trust has been lost. But if I did it, then so can you.

I love my own company today and am content in my life. I receive a lot of love externally, but the most important love is my love for myself. I invite you to open the door to love and use this affirmation to affirm with me, "I am lovable."

I am not broken.

When I found myself at The Recovery Ranch in drug and alcohol treatment for the second time, I felt broken beyond repair. I had made a mess of my life with two years of crack and IV drug use, followed by a suicide attempt. I hit rock bottom and did not know how to heal, stay sober, and create a life in which I did not want to use. I never thought I would stop drinking, but with a lot of hard work and many hours in the rooms of AA, I eventually did.

For the first time, I understood how the trauma underlying my addictions kept me from staying sober. I met teachers and guides at The Ranch that helped me to see that trauma is a healthy response to a horrible situation and that we have the power to find even better responses when we're ready. Those teachers guided my healing and walked with me through some challenging times.

They pointed me toward other teachers and life experiences that would heal and grow me. With their help, I changed my belief system, and I no longer feel broken.

Another gift from my time at The Ranch was the introduction of yoga into my life. It made me feel good when I felt pretty rotten. Yoga means "union" or "to yoke together," so I see it as a kind of integration. Yoga brought the unloved pieces of me into the light where they could heal and be loved. Yoga has integrated my parts and pieces into the whole of who I am now.

Yoga also gave me God and a spirituality that works for me. There is still work to do, but my trauma no longer runs my life. Through yoga, I learned how to let loss and the feelings it brings break the walls and armor around my heart. Every time I fall to my knees in pain -- from the loss of my brother Robby twenty-three years ago to the loss of my Dad, the recent loss of my brother Bill, and all the other losses in between -- my heart breaks open a little more. Every time I hit bottom -- and there have been many times -- God caught me in the net of support and love that was my family and friends.

I have turned my broken places into strengths, and I know you can too. You can integrate your unloved parts and pieces into wholeness as you learn to love yourself. I invite you to close your eyes, take a deep breath, and tell yourself, "I love you." Wrap your arms around yourself while doing that, and tell yourself these three things: "I am good enough. I am loveable. And I am not broken."

Self Portrait '90

Creativity has saved my life. There are so many ways that I am creative. Teaching yoga is a creative process for me, as I don't always know what I will do next; I must rely on my intuition and my body to guide me. I was a photographer before I became a yogi, and I enjoyed the creative process of taking photographs and developing film and prints in the darkroom. I've also had to be creative in my life to medicate the pain of unhealed trauma. I discovered many addictive ways to feel better, different, or numb. I had to be creative to get my needs met in codependent relationships that were abusive at times. I had to be creative to manage multiple addictions while trying to function. The consequences were terrible, but these solutions kept me alive until I could own my creativity and find better solutions.

I had to be even more creative with my recovery. My recovery journey started thirty years ago in the rooms of AA and ACOA but expanded further when I came to The Recovery Ranch in middle Tennessee. A whole new world opened up with the addition of the book "The Four Agreements" by Don Miguel Ruiz, the Toltec Path, Native American sweat lodge, the medicine wheel, and yoga. I co-created and lived in the intentional community of Laughing Winds, building a life and a family around these teachings and ceremonies.

I have not always done as I was advised, but I made each of these teachings my own as I tried to follow my internal compass. For the most part, I have done a great job of creating a life that I love and a solid and healthy recovery. My life is full of magic and miracles.

Are you afraid to be creative because you think whatever you do or make won't be good enough? Do you do creative things? Creativity comes in many different ways, not just artistically. We can be creative loading the dishwasher or doodling. We can be creative with food. Every task can be creative, and we all have a creative spark inside of us. I invite you to think about all the ways you are creative in your life. Every choice you make creates the fabric of your life. Make choices that make you happy. Remember that practice makes the master. Each new choice can raise the vibration of your creativity. Affirm your creativity and say the affirmation like a mantra. Be open, curious, and patient, and see what happens. Recognize the creativity in your own life, use it now, and affirm with me, "I am creative."

I am unique.

There is only one of me in all creation, and I came into this world as a unique ray of light -- as we all do! -- with gifts to share with the world that are personal to me. My stories are different from yours, but many of my experiences, feelings, and life lessons might be the same.

The life I have lived from birth until now has been extraordinary. I experienced trauma as a child, addiction, and alcoholism as an adult, and I "hit bottom" more than once. I have known a few dark nights of the soul, and I have known a lot of happiness as well. I have had to do the hard work of living my truth as a gay man in a world that wasn't always as accepting as it is now, and that has at times been hard. I can finally celebrate the challenges as well as the successes, because all of these have molded me into the unique person I am today.

I believe it is our uniqueness that makes us special, that makes us powerful. Without the trauma and the healing I've experienced, I might be a less patient, compassionate, and courageous man. Both the negative and the positive things have molded me into the person I am today. I am so grateful to say that I love myself today, and I love the life I have created. So much of my story has been written in these memes. It is a story of hard work, miracles, and a whole lot of grace.

Are you constantly judging yourself and comparing yourself to others? Are you critical of the things that make you different? Sometimes we trauma survivors want to blend in, as we are used to being invisible. I invite you to step into the light and be proud of everything that makes you different from others. I am so grateful that we are all different from each other. Let us come together and tell each other our stories, find our commonality, and learn from our differences instead of being afraid of what we don't know or understand. I invite you to celebrate those parts of you that make you unique. Each one of us can make our uniqueness a gift to us all. Please join me by affirming the gift of your own uniqueness with the affirmation, "I am unique."

I am strong.

Strength comes in many forms, so it's important to recognize the kind of strength that is our own. My definition of "strength" – the one that helps me recognize and grow my own strength -- is the ability to keep showing up, no matter what challenges or obstacles are in the way.

I was a sensitive child and appeared more fragile than I really was. My childhood and teenage years were hard at times, but I survived being sent to a boarding school halfway around the world, crying myself to sleep, sexual abuse, teasing, and bullying. I learned to toughen up, and I learned to cultivate discipline. I developed tremendous strength, determination, and resilience. These qualities saved me in times of depression and carried me through addiction, cancer, and chronic pain.

Yoga has taken these strengths to a whole new level. Yoga has grown a strength in me that is not only physical but mental and spiritual as well. A daily yoga practice gave me meditation and my breath, and it has grown my ability to change the channel of my attention from suffering to gratitude. I have cultivated a deep trust in God and the benevolence of the Universe. Though my life challenges started early, I have found it is true that what didn't kill me made me stronger.

I invite you to take a moment and think of all your strengths and the ways that you are strong. Consider the strength that has come out of your tears and pain; the strength to just keep showing up when you can hardly get out of bed, grieving the death of a loved one; the strength of caring for a sick child or elderly parent; the strength it takes to pick yourself up after losing a job; the strength it takes to share your pain with another person honesty and authentically; the strength it takes to ask for help when you've hit rock bottom; and the strength it takes to live in integrity and do hard things. These examples only scratch the surface of strength. Our struggles strengthen and grow us.

Acknowledging all of my strengths makes me wonder why I am ever afraid! Of course, I am human, so I forget and get afraid sometimes – but then I discover that I am strong even when I am afraid. I invite you to join me in recognizing your strengths with gratitude and affirming, "I am strong."

I am a survivor on many levels. I have survived cancer, alcoholism, crack, and IV drug addiction. I am also a survivor of sexual abuse and other childhood trauma, and I have lived for many years with mental health issues. Looking back now, I can see more clearly how I survived all of these things; I was given a strong body, an intelligent mind, a resilient heart, and substantial inner resources to make it to this, my 61st year.

God and community have been important parts of my survival. I have been in recovery for thirty years and have worked hard to create a sober and healthy life. God blessed me at every turn and dead end along the way. There have been some very deep holes that I didn't know how I was going to climb out of, but I have always had the care and support I needed to keep showing up. I even tried to end my life twice, but a web of love held me, made of family, friends, and the grace of God that surrounds me always.

I survived in spite of all my doubts; I didn't think I would live this long. If you had told me at age twenty what life challenges were around the corner and down the road, I wouldn't have been very hopeful that I would make it. I have overcome and survived more than I ever thought I could have. Today I am thriving in the life I have created with a man I love deeply, and I am doing work with my yoga ministry that nourishes my soul and spirit daily.

What are your stories of survival? I believe that it is true that God doesn't give us more than we can handle and that what doesn't kill us makes us stronger. I don't know what it's like to walk in your shoes or what your challenges are, but I do know that we don't get through this life without hardship and tears. I also know that those tears grow compassion and wisdom. I invite you to reflect on what you have survived and overcome and how it has strengthened you. Affirm that you have the strength to continue to meet life's challenges as they come. I don't know what is down the road from here, but I know that I am strong, and God hasn't dropped me yet. I am blessed. I invite you to affirm with me, "I am a survivor."

In honor of World AIDS Day, the time has come for me to share with you that I have been living with HIV and AIDS for thirty-two years – over half of my life. I see resilience as adaptability in the face of challenge, and HIV has been my biggest life challenge. I tested positive in 1989 in the early days of the AIDS epidemic, and I thought I would be dead in a year since many weren't living much longer. My body had to adapt to different medications and their side effects. My mind was filled with the fear of a cough or a sore throat. My heart felt shame and the fear of judgment, which kept me from sharing this until now. It has been a long journey, complicated by addiction and alcoholism. I developed AIDS-related lymphoma in 2005, and it took two years to recover from the chemotherapy. Cancer was rough and contributed to the chronic pain that is my constant companion.

I did recover, though, and I will stay in remission as long as I take my HIV meds. Yoga and clean living keep me healthy - mentally, physically, spiritually, and emotionally. You have read many affirmations about the challenges I have overcome: healing trauma, recovering from cancer, anxiety, depression, various addictions, self-harm, and seeing myself through the eyes of terrible self-hate. My journey as a gay man taught me a lot about survival, including how to be resilient in a judgmental and sometimes homophobic world. Learning how to cope with my HIV status, and my journey with AIDS, underlie them all. I have always felt God guiding me, holding me, and keeping me safe on my journey, as Jesus does in the poem, "Footsteps in the Sand." There were many times I have had to be carried.

This is a powerful truth that I have kept hidden for so long. I choose to no longer carry around the shame of my HIV+ status. I choose to shine in my incredible story of survival. I am proud of my resilience and the inner resources that keep me showing up despite the mental health issues that once kept me living in fear. Life with HIV and AIDS is easier today. I am no longer afraid of a cold, and the medications, though prohibitively expensive, are free of side effects and keep the virus undetectable in my body, unable to spread to others. Now I am free.

Do you believe that you aren't strong? Are you facing challenges that you can't see your way through? I invite you to look at your own resilience, recognize the things you have overcome, and see how you have adapted to your challenges in an ever-changing world. I invite you to recognize the internal resources that kept you moving forward and the support of God in your life that allowed you to get up and dust yourself off again and again. Please join me in affirming our common resilience as we face the future and move forward together. Join me in affirming, "I am resilient."

I am grateful to be alive.

I have known many dark nights of the soul and I have been close to death multiple times. Times when I didn't necessarily want to die, when I just couldn't see my way forward and I didn't know how to ask for help. I have struggled with depression most of my life. Sometimes I wanted to die when life became too hard, and I didn't have any hope. I tried to take my life twice. I took so many risks and put myself in dangerous situations so casually. I was in so much pain I tried pretty much anything that would take me out of myself or numb me out. I pushed the envelope, flirting with death every time – all the while telling myself, "I don't care what happens to me." I went into the darkness so many times, and every time, I emerged like a phoenix from the ashes.

Fortunately, the memories of those hard times and dark nights of the soul are just whispers in the dark now. I have been blessed with the resources to get help when I need it. I always said yes, and my family never gave up on me. I surrounded myself with people who were modeling health, stability, sobriety, and self-love. I had awesome teachers and therapists. God supported me at every turn and opened many doors. I just had to say yes and walk through them. I worked hard, and I am living a life I would have never thought possible, loving myself more than I ever thought I could.

Have you had times when you didn't want to be alive? Times when you were in despair and had lost all hope? I hope that if you are in that place right now, you find encouragement in my words. Things can get better. Once you decide to start the journey of recovery and healing, I believe Life will support you in ways that are both visible and invisible. Ask for help from someone safe. There are 12-step meetings for any addiction, and they can show us that God does for us what we can't do for ourselves. Help comes in so many forms. It helps to have an open mind and be teachable. We can heal. We can stay sober. We can thrive. You can create a God of your understanding and your own spirituality. I am so glad I am still here. If you have stood at the edge of a cliff and are here today, and even if you haven't, I invite you to join me in affirming, "I am grateful to be alive."

Section III : Stretching My Wings

Gratitude is a gateway to freedom.

Anyone who has ever been in one of my workshops or yoga classes knows how much I speak about gratitude. It is the first question I ask my students when I start a class and my most frequent prayer. Gratitude connects us to the present moment, each other, and our appreciation and love. When I find myself in a mental or emotional state that I would rather not be in, such as anxiety, sadness, or anger, I can often shift out of that state by redirecting my attention to something I am grateful for. This simple shift can literally "change the channel" of my emotional experience. It may not be easy to find something I'm grateful for in the midst of suffering, but I can always find something. I just have to practice recognizing it. There may be other times when I want to hang on to my suffering, and that's okay too. I can choose!

Practicing gratitude has transformed my life, even in my darkest times. When I was recovering from cancer and chemotherapy and was too depressed to get out of bed, I still made gratitude lists morning and night. These lists made me aware of the blessing of being alive, my medicine, and my doctors. I started off with naming only a few things and worked my way up to ten. It wasn't always easy, but I stuck with it, and I believe it helped lift my depression. I was always able to find something to be grateful for. Gratitude also connects me to God. I am aware every day that I am a miracle, having survived death multiple times.

We live with many luxuries we take for granted, like drinkable water out of the tap and hot showers. Some of us have change in a jar on our dresser, which may not be much to us but might be wealth to a starving child in a third-world country. The next time you're in an emotional place you'd rather not be in, I invite you to try practicing gratitude. Take a moment and think about what you are grateful for, the little things and the big things, even the people we love that get on our nerves and challenge us. Take a few deep mindful breaths and see how your mood has shifted. I invite you to affirm with me, "Gratitude is a gateway to freedom."

I have always had a relationship with God, though it has morphed and changed over the years. As a child, I went to church with my family and sang in the choir. I thought as a child: I believed that if I was a good Christian, bad things wouldn't happen. Then I experienced the trauma of my mother's aneurism, sexual abuse, the guilt and shame of being gay, and the loss of my best friend to suicide when I was 17. I leaned heavily on my Christian faith and prayed ceaselessly, but it didn't stop these traumas from continuing to happen. God couldn't change the fact that I was gay. I felt rejected by the church for being gay. I felt abandoned by God. I was just a child. My faith was shaken over and over again, but I never stopped believing. I just could not understand.

Things began to change in my 20's. I found I could expand the way I thought about God as I voraciously read Shirley Maclaine's books. The way she talked about spirituality, reincarnation, and energy made sense to me. She gave me permission to think about God in a new way, and she became a model for creating my own spirituality. Around the same time, I started attending AA, and I was encouraged to do the same in my program of recovery.

Yoga, Toltec, and Native American teachings expanded and deepened my understanding of God even more. I go to church regularly today, but my beliefs about God are much bigger than what happens there. Spirituality and religion aren't the same for me, and my relationship with Mother/Father God is bigger than I can put words to. Today I experience God as an impersonal benevolent creator of the Universe, a powerful source of Life with which I can have a personal relationship.

Aging has also grown me spiritually. Overcoming many challenges has deepened my faith. Every time I've fallen to my knees in despair, God has been there to help me get up and keep going. In recovery, I have learned that the only way to stay sober is to trust in God to do for me what I can't do myself and help me live my life one hour, one day at a time.

We all share a divine spark, whether or not we are aware of it. How we tend to that spark is a lifetime's journey; spirituality is a personal thing. There are many paths to the top of the mountain; how we climb, when we climb, the way we climb, or even if we choose not to climb is all our choice. We are the architects of our lives.

I invite you to think about your spirituality. What makes your heart and spirit feel alive? To some, being in a forest is church, or in my father's case, being out on the water. Call it what you like, God, Spirit, Universe, Jesus, higher self, or whatever works for you. If you are happy with your relationship with God and your spirituality already works for you, great! The bottom line is that it's your life, and you can create your own spirituality. Spend some time in Nature, or find some quiet time in your day, even if it is only for a few minutes. Find what lifts your heart and gives your soul life. Open your mind and heart and explore a new relationship with the God of your understanding. I invite you to join me in affirming, "I create my own spirituality."

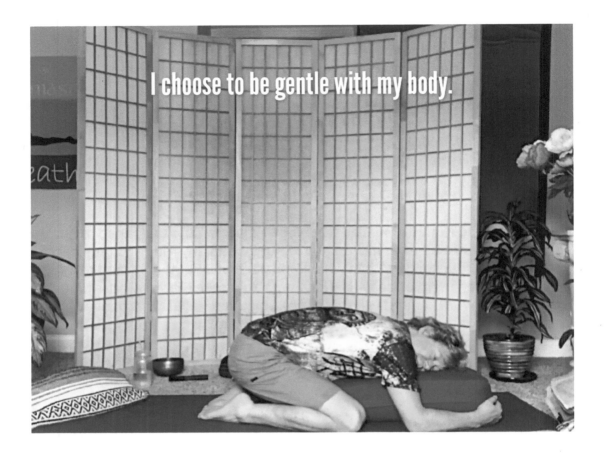

I choose to be gentle with my body.

I have spent my life rushing around and pushing my body whenever I have the opportunity, even when I teach yoga. I have been practicing and teaching yoga for twenty years. While it has healed me on so many levels, it has also fed my addiction to intensity. I am a shy introvert who sits in front of people almost daily and does what does not come naturally to me. I may sparkle and shine outwardly, but on the inside, I am on autopilot because I am anxious. When I am anxious, I make the movements faster and more difficult. Since anxiety is my usual state, this has been very hard on my body because I can't turn the intensity down. Full tilt is my normal when I teach. I am living with chronic pain from this general 'overdoing,' not restricted to my yoga mat. It is the same with house and yard chores or pretty much anything I do. It is my goal as a yoga teacher to please, and I have big ideas about what I think my students want.

I recently celebrated my 61st birthday. I never thought I would make it this far, as I self-destructed with the same passion I put into overachieving, so my body is in rough shape. I am concerned about my limitations and challenges if I live to be 80. The good news is that I know how to use yoga to heal myself. The challenge is that I am having trouble making the required internal shift. The shift is in learning how to teach gentleness – which is what I myself need – and trusting that it will be good for whoever is in front of me. I have to trust that it isn't just the movement my students come for. They come for the same reason I teach, to be spiritually nourished. I do not want to give up my yoga ministry. Teaching yoga sustains me and gives my life purpose.

Practicing gentleness is a choice. It doesn't come easy to me, but my body requires it, or I will not be able to keep doing what I love. When I take care of myself, I take care of my students. It's time to teach by example how to 'be' instead of 'do.' Asking for help is not a weakness; it's a superpower. I give up striving, overachieving and over-doing and trust whatever I do is more than good enough.

With the stress of life as we know it today, we need to step off of the hamster wheel, slow down, and be gentle with our precious bodies. We are programmed early to work hard and give 110%. I choose to let go of the belief that I think I know what you want and need. I let go of the belief that my self-love depends on your happiness. I no longer have to work so hard to be loved by myself.

Do you push yourself hard at the expense of your body? Is your over-achieving catching up with you? Do you live with chronic pain? Many of my students are my age or older. We are seniors. If all this pushing is hard on me, what's it like for them? This affirmation snuck in under the wire during the editing process and may be the most important one I am using now in my life. I need this affirmation, and I am guessing some of you might need it too. We are all tired of the approval-seeking, over-achieving, and other behaviors that have worked for us in the past but that are harming us now. Our bodies tell us to slow down and give them some love and attention. Modern medicine keeps us alive often longer than our expiration date. All this pushing will catch up with us. I encourage you to listen to your body and practice gentleness. Listen to your exhaustion, pain, and tiredness; listen to when your body is telling you to step back, turn down the intensity, and rest. Give your body plenty of water, fresh air, healthy food, laughter, tenderness, rest, and most of all, love. Join me in affirming, "I choose to be gentle with my body."

I relax my grip.

Life in an alcoholic household was at times like riding a rollercoaster; there were periods of happiness and calm, and there were moments of terror. I experienced multiple traumas early in my life, which set me up for a life of addiction, and the need to control and micromanage every part of it. My mind tells me if I can control something, I can keep myself safe. In trying to prevent bad things, I miss out on the possibility of good things happening. Perfectionism and approval-seeking have kept my grip tight on the wheel as I have tried to do my best to keep myself safe by ensuring I was good enough and lovable.

It has always been much easier for me to surrender the big things I know I have no control over. Most things I am afraid of don't turn out to be that bad. It's the little things that are hard to let go of. There are some things I can control, like the words that come out of my mouth, but there is so much I can't control, like people and their actions. It's helpful to be able to discern which is which.

Yoga has given me tools to manage the anxiety that has me gripping the wheel tight, and I have learned to trust God/Life /Universe. Trying to control everything can be like paddling against the current; it can take and waste a lot of energy. I have learned that God does for me what I cannot do myself, and things always turn out better than I could have managed myself.

Are you tired of micromanaging your life and the people around you? Can you relax easily and simply 'be' without the need to do something? Do you feel anxious when you are not in control of a situation? I invite you to create some space in your life to be still and connect to your breath and your gratitude. Look for the times in your past when spontaneity and taking risks led to something good. I have found that things always work out better when I surrender them and get out of the way of God working in my life. I invite you to trust God to work in yours and take more risks. Good things happen when we let go of our fear. Join me in affirming," I relax my grip."

I take my foot off the gas.

Addiction, for me, is a many-headed Hydra. Each head represents a different addiction: work, sex, drugs, alcohol, and the many other things I used to numb the pain I carried inside. Recovery has been, at times, like playing 'whack-a-mole' with sobriety. In the thirty years I have been in recovery, I have had many periods of sobriety from particular addictions, but not always at the same time. The common denominator to all of them, though, is an overarching addiction to intensity: I tend to press down hard on the gas.

I was a sensitive child and felt things deeply. I was traumatized in multiple ways. I was not equipped to process all the intense emotions I was feeling; abandonment, shame, guilt, anger, fear, loneliness, and an ever-present sadness and anxiety. I lived with an ever-present intensity that kept my nervous system in a state of arousal – which I became addicted to. My whole life became focused on pleasing people and seeking approval, pushing myself hard in whatever I was doing. Perfectionism, over-achieving, and intensity walk hand in hand together.

I need to use this affirmation because I still push myself too hard, rushing around and ignoring various injuries. This pushing has left me with chronic pain, anxiety, depletion, and even speeding tickets. I must take my foot off the gas, put on the brake, and slow down. To balance out my need for intensity, I spend a lot of time in peace and quiet. I have made my home a sanctuary and created a simple life that nourishes me deeply. Yoga is a good fit for me as well, as it satisfies my need for intensity while also balancing that out with the peace that comes from restorative yoga and meditation. Working with my breath calms me down. Every day yoga teaches me how to dial back the need for intensity.

Do you numb yourself out because you feel things so intensely? Do you put yourself in dangerous situations or take risks casually? Is your life out of balance? Are you able to relax and be still? I invite you to look at your relationship to intensity. Most addicts are addicted to intensity because it makes us feel alive and medicates our pain at the same time. If a behavior makes you feel good and doesn't harm you, enjoy it, but if it makes you feel shame or guilt or hurts you, it might be time to do something about it. Find a practice like yoga that teaches non-harming and non-judgment. Find what works for you and give yourself permission to slow down. I invite you to turn back the dial on your need for intensity and join me in affirming, "I take my foot off the gas."

I give up my image of perfection.

This affirmation is still a big one for me, as perfectionism sometimes finds its way into my life even now – especially when I think I know what others want and expect of me. I raise the bar higher and higher, making myself feel "not good enough" and unlovable every time I don't measure up to my expectations. I put so much pressure on myself to get it right and then judge myself when I believe I haven't.

It is good that I want to be the best human and teacher I can be, but it is not good that I use that ideal against myself instead of using it to inspire me. I have spent so much of my life judging myself and comparing myself with others, even to the point of self-hatred and self-harm.

Thankfully, I have aged a little, done a lot of work on myself, and changed my belief system to a more compassionate one. Now, I know that whatever I do is my best, and my best is more than good enough. I love myself so much today that I see my fear, judgments, anxiety, and humanity, and find myself so very perfect just the way I am. I believe it is our imperfections that make us interesting. I can relax, breathe, and stop trying so hard. I allow myself to be more of a human being today than a human doing.

We live in a world of instant information and connection. Wherever we look, social media and advertising encourage us to buy anything that will make us look or feel perfect, attractive, and therefore good enough and loveable. These images of perfection are unattainable and only lead to more pressure and suffering. This pressure creates self-judgment, which creates self-hatred and self-punishment. Think about all the pressure you put on yourself, and notice how much energy it wastes, how much judgment, self-hatred, and punishment it creates for you. Do you want to give up the pressure to be perfect? Stop believing the lies that tell you you're not perfect the way you are without all this striving and pressure. Use this affirmation like a mantra and notice when you are pressuring yourself to be perfect. Practicing compassion and self-forgiveness are key to working with this affirmation. We have to stop being so hard on ourselves and forgive ourselves when we do. Life is messy sometimes. I invite you to stop raising the bar on yourself and shine your light just as you are. Explore giving voice to your authentic self, and affirm with me, "I give up my image of perfection."

I forgive myself.

I forgive myself for every time I've judged myself, found myself guilty, and punished myself. I forgive myself for lying, stealing, hurting my family and friends, and for abandoning myself when I needed myself the most. I forgive myself for hurting my body through overwork, addiction, and trying to take my life. Most of all, I forgive myself for every time I have held myself up to a false image of perfection in order to find myself good enough and worthy of love.

I have been so hard on myself, and it's taken a long time to reach this place of forgiveness. We often forgive ourselves last, but we need to be the first because we are the most important ones we need to forgive. When we don't forgive ourselves, we punish ourselves, which keeps us from loving ourselves or anyone else.

I have found peace in my heart by forgiving the people who hurt me and caused me pain, so now I give myself the same grace. I no longer want to punish myself for not being perfect. I may never forget the harm done to me or by me, but with forgiveness, I can be free to move on from the pain they caused. Every moment of my life, the good, the bad, and the ugly, has brought me to today, and today I love myself, and I love my life.

Do you withhold love and forgiveness from yourself? Are you hard on yourself? Do you hold yourself up to an image of perfection? Do you suffer every time you remember an offense you've committed against someone or that has been done to you? I invite you to open up your heart and let yourself off the hook. We were doing our best with what we had to work with.

I invite you to bring all your parts into the light of your love, especially those you have the greatest trouble loving. Forgiveness is a path to self-love, and self-love is a path to God. I invite you to stop judging and start loving, add a little forgiveness and join me in affirming, "I forgive myself."

I forgive myself for not being able to forgive.

At one point in my recovery, I discovered a part of me, contracted from trauma, that had created a wall I hadn't even known was there. I knew that many other walls in my life were no longer there, so the odds were in my favor that this one, with my effort and God's grace, would fall away too. I prayed to God that my heart would soften around my inability to forgive and that this wall would melt away with the sun of my loving. I knew that I am brave and that I can do hard things. Even the fact that I was at this point, facing such a big wall, indicated that I was taking another leap of growth! I knew something else about walls; they are there to protect. When we have walls around our hearts, there is always something precious on the other side of them yet to be discovered.

This wall, like all the others, did eventually begin to melt away.

What walls are you facing in your life? Do you judge yourself because you can't get past them? Do you judge yourself because you have them? Can you recognize the progress that got you to where you are? Moving through a wall can be something like eating an elephant, one small bite at a time.

It's okay if you can't forgive. It takes time and safety. Let yourself off the hook and trust that you have been doing your best, and your best is good enough. Trust that you are where you need to be and trust the value of your own walls.

We do not need to be perfect to be lovable. I invite you to take a breath with me and trust in the power of love and trust in the process of healing. It's okay if you can't forgive just yet. I've invited you to trust a lot, and it's okay if you can't do that either. It will happen in its own time. Open your heart, find some gratitude, and join me in affirming, "I forgive myself for not being able to forgive."

I will keep showing up.
I will not give up.

Once in adventure therapy, I climbed a telephone pole and stood by myself on the top of a 12"x12" platform. What a fantastic feeling that was; doing something I wouldn't have thought possible. I showed up. I didn't give up. With the encouragement of my community on the ground below, shouting up at me, I conquered my fear and discovered that I was truly supported in my life. This experience showed me that I truly needed help, and with that help, I could create a solid foundation for my recovery.

I guess the biggest thing that brought me to where I am today is that I just keep showing up, no matter what. When I originally wrote this a couple of years ago, I was getting ready for major back surgery. It was the next thing I had to show up for, and I was anxious about it.

Things were very different for a while as I recovered. It was a challenge to bounce back from, but it also became a portal to a new, improved version of myself. The loves, likes, and inspirational comments I received through social media nourished my spirit and reminded me I wasn't alone, and I could do this with support. My surgery was successful, and I am no longer living with back pain. Because of years of yoga practice, I healed quickly and was back at work sooner than I thought. I may not be able to see too far ahead into the future, but I kept putting one foot in front of the other, trusting God to guide me and Life to support me as I did the next right thing.

I invite you to keep moving forward one step at a time, "eating the elephant" of the difficult situations in your life one bite at a time and showing up in your life one hour or minute at a time. Think about times in your life you got through, whether gracefully or with difficulty. See the ways you were supported by God through other people. Let this show you that you were not alone, and that you were able to get through the hard times by showing up and taking one step at a time. Give yourself praise for moving forward into situations that require you to go out of your comfort zone and make hard decisions. I invite you to believe in yourself and join me in affirming, "I will keep showing up. I will not give up."

My story has value.

For most of my life, I felt my story was a sad one because I focused on the pain and suffering of unhealed trauma. It wasn't a story I liked to share. As I age, I can see more of the bigger picture and why some things had to happen to me to make me into the man I love today. My story is nothing short of a miracle. Things I used to see as painful are now markers for my growth and evolution.

As I learned how to love myself, it changed how I tell my story. I began to share what I have overcome and accomplished, hoping that it might benefit or inspire someone else who might be struggling with the same issues and challenges. I began to share how I have tried to follow my inner compass and chosen my own path and how that has worked for me. I shared how I have grown and healed in these last 20 years through a mix of 12-step recovery, the Toltec teachings of Don Miguel Ruiz, Native American teachings and practices, co-creating and living in the intentional community of Laughing Winds, and teaching yoga. I share how much I love the life I have created and the people I share it with.

I am so grateful to be alive, and I am so grateful that my story is, for the most part, one of triumph over challenge. I have walked into the darkness many times and have returned a battered but much wiser man.

The details and challenges of my life differ from yours, but some of the feelings and underlying issues might be the same. Our stories have so much value. They connect us to each other. They heal us. We each have a story to tell and unique gifts to share. We find commonality in our shared stories. We learn from each other, and we never know how our story will positively impact another. I invite you to trust that your story has value, share it with someone safe, and affirm with me, "My story has value."

I can change my story.

Many of the stories I used to tell myself were sad ones. Early childhood trauma and thirty years of drug and alcohol addiction created a lot of drama and suffering in my life. That story began to change in 2002 when I was given "The Four Agreements" by Don Miguel Ruiz as I checked into treatment at The Recovery Ranch in middle Tennessee. That book led to twenty years of work and personal growth, exploring his teachings and making many trips down to the ancient pyramid city of Teotihuacan, Mexico.

During the years since I met Don Miguel, under the guidance of his many teachers, I learned how to look at my life and the stories I tell about it through the eyes of love and compassion instead of the eyes of judgment and fear. I have learned to reexamine my points of view about people and experiences that have caused me pain. I discovered that there is gold in our moments of pain: they help us reach for help, connect with God, and experience God's grace. I changed my stories in many ways: I wrote them out to see what was true and what was not, I examined my beliefs, and I mined the gold in my own stories. I recognized the stories that fueled my sadness and focused on better ones.

Though most days my glass is overflowing, sometimes it's definitely half empty – but even on those days, my stories about myself are of love, gratitude, contentment, compassion, and resilience. I have everything I need and want, and I am happy. Thank you to all my teachers and to Don Miguel Ruiz for teaching me how to change my story. Doing that ultimately changed my life. I am no longer walking around with a cloud of sadness over my head. I feel so much freer and happier since I changed my story.

What stories are you telling yourself today? Do they uplift you or cause you to feel anxiety, guilt, or shame? If you want to change some of your stories, it begins with awareness of the stories you are telling and how they make you feel. Discern what is fact and what is fiction. So much of our pain comes from what we tell ourselves. I invite you to refocus your attention and look for the good that has happened in your life instead. Think about changing the stories that are judgmental and cause you unhappiness. Negative stories steal our energy. If I can do it, you can do it too. Join me in affirming, "I can change my story."

Every choice I make creates the masterpiece
that is my life.

Life is about choices. We create our lives with every single choice we make. A wise man once told me a very simple thing. Make a choice and pay attention to the feedback. If you don't like the feedback make another choice, but without judgment. I have learned that all the tiny little choices are the foundations of the bigger ones. I am grateful for all the choices I have made, good and bad, for they have brought me to where I am, and I love my life. My life was created by millions of choices, many big, but mostly small. Even though my life was painful at times, it led me to where I am; and when I saw through eyes that were clear of self-judgment and self-hatred, I could see the beauty and the possibility of healing behind the pain. My survival and my story of healing are a masterpiece.

Do you believe you create your reality? Do you find it hard to see your life as a masterpiece? It's hard to see it when you're in your suffering – but when you can step out of it and see with different eyes, you can have appreciation and compassion toward your healing journey. Think about how your choices have brought you to where you are, reading this book right now, and how these affirmations resonate with you. I hope they inspire you to change your perspective a little, be more authentic, and say yes to Life. I believe every choice we make matters – even the smallest ones.

Our lives are our art. What do you want to create? If you don't like your creation, you can start over as many times as you like. Every day can be a new start, a blank canvas. What is your next brushstroke, note, or word going to be? What is the next choice that will bring you closer to authenticity?

I invite you to make your choices consciously with awareness and intention, even the little ones. We are each sending a vibration out into the Universe, and the Universe responds to that vibration. I believe that choices that come out of love rather than fear, out of our gratitude, attract more to us of what we are grateful for. Please acknowledge with me, " Every choice I make creates the masterpiece that is my life."

Section IV : Trusting Myself to Fly

Gratitude is my foundation.

I have had some peak, top-of-the-mountain experiences in my life, and I have also been suicidal and filled with despair. There were many dark nights of the soul and many self-destructive dead ends. My path has not been an easy one. I have survived much, and I have overcome many challenges that I never thought possible. I have been blessed with many miracles and second chances on my recovery journey. I believe that the pain and suffering I have experienced have given me some wisdom and made me a more compassionate man. I am grateful for all the challenges I have survived, including cancer, alcoholism, and addiction. I am also grateful for the life I have created, the people in it, and the soul-fulfilling work I do with my yoga ministry. I have known hardship, so I appreciate the luxuries, abundance, and freedoms I enjoy today.

I believe the Universe responds to the vibration we send out, and I believe that if I send out a vibration of gratitude and love, it will attract more of what I am grateful for. "Like attracts like" is a Universal Law. I expect magic and miracles in my life every day because they happen so often. I also find that practicing gratitude keeps me in the present moment, where I experience life's magic. I try to live and teach from a place of service, and I am showered with blessing and abundance at every turn. When I talk with God, my prayers are not so much petitions, but simply to say thank you.

There are four affirmations in this book that are devoted to gratitude. It is a gift that keeps on giving. I invite you to think of all the things and people you take for granted in your life. I invite you to share your gratitude with the people you love. Tell them how much you appreciate them. Things could always be worse, so there is always something to be grateful for. Find gratitude for the simple things in your life and feel your heart soften around your resentments and self-judgment. Build your life on a firm foundation of gratitude. Practice gratitude and watch your life transform. Join me in affirming, "Gratitude is my foundation."

I trust the process of healing my life.

There were three days in the hospital after my back surgery when my pain was too great to be managed. It was absolute hell, but I made it through, and just two weeks later, I was in a space of healing that was nothing short of miraculous! These affirmations supported me as I patiently rested and encouraged my body to heal. In the bigger picture, I was healing more than just my physical body. I learned to ask for help. I learned to be patient and rest, and I learned not to overdo it. I realized I have the inner resources to get through things I never imagined.

I also learned how supported I was in my healing process. I had rooms full of fellow addicts and alcoholics in AA who made me feel less alone when I came to meetings. I had the community of Laughing Winds, my family of choice, who surrounded me with love and cared for me when I was recovering from cancer, as well as some great therapists, doctors, and counselors. I have solid family support and friends who I call 'lifelines.' I also have my partner Teddy who walks beside me, holds my hand, and provides unconditional love and a safe haven. God has supported me through all of these people. My prayers are always answered.

Healing anything is a process. It is not always linear, and it takes the time it takes, which is not often on our schedule. Many of us can get impatient on our journey towards health, integration, and wholeness. Our bodies often heal more quickly than the heart and mind when traumatized. Sometimes we take three steps forward and two steps back. I have found that breakthroughs along the way are wonderful, but it's the slow, steady, one foot in front of the other that reaches the goal. We can trust the ups and downs and trust that we are right where we need to be, doing what we need to be doing to heal.

What needs healing in your life? I invite you to recognize that healing is a process, and I invite you to trust that process. I invite you to see yourself supported, loved, cared for, and guided. When we set our intention to heal, I believe Life conspires to support us in so many ways. Open up your heart and your mind to this affirmation and say with me, "I trust the process of healing my life."

I trust myself to meet the unknown.

There is a place I go to in the ancient city of Teotihuacan, Mexico, high on top of the pyramid of Quetzalcoatl, that we call the leap of faith. Two thousand years ago apprentices would demonstrate faith in life by literally running into the darkness and jumping from the top of the pyramid. They did not know there was water below to catch them. I have taken that symbolic leap so many times over the last two decades. Doing that has helped me cultivate the trust I now have in myself to meet life, whatever the challenge is. I do not know what is around the corner, but I have discovered that I have a record of showing up, adapting, and making solid, healthy choices even in the face of life's greatest challenges.

When I left my last treatment center twelve years ago, I was all set to go to an Intensive Outpatient Treatment and follow the sensible advice of my counselors and friends. Instead, I chose to go to yoga school and get my certification. It was a real fork-in-the-road choice point in my life, where I didn't know which way to go; I even had my first panic attack trying to figure it out. Even though I had already been teaching for years, cancer left my body weak, and I didn't know if I could physically do the training.

It wasn't easy, but everything inside me knew I had to do this. I trusted myself to meet the unknown. I followed my inner guidance and chose yoga. I deepened my practice, and it saved my life. Teaching yoga has given my life purpose and helped me create a life I love.

Yoga gave me the tools to face my life with a solid grounding. We take strength, balance, and flexibility off the mat and into our lives. Yoga teaches us to raise our energy and our vibration, and to hold on to that energy so that we can stay centered when life comes to blow us off course.

I invite you to affirm your strength and power. Think of all the things you have accomplished and the trials you have overcome to get to this moment. I am sure there were times you didn't think you would make it, but here you are. There are many unknowns in the world, and we can get stressed out thinking about them and what's possibly around the corner, but we can also trust that God will take care of us. He hasn't dropped us yet. Take a leap of faith and join me in affirming, "I trust myself to meet the unknown."

Life speaks to me. I listen.

Yoga has helped me become a better listener. It has expanded my awareness physically, mentally, and emotionally. I listen to life with all of my senses. Information comes from the outside world and from inside of me. My body is always giving me information, telling me how I feel, when I am safe or in danger, awake or sleepy, hot or cold, well or sick, sad or happy. I pay attention to my inner guidance as well. Sometimes I need to be quiet to hear it, but I also get intuitive hits while mowing the lawn, blowing leaves, doing house chores, buying groceries, or resting on the floor in savasana.

I pay attention to synchronicities. I often look at my phone just as it says 1:11 or 11:11, or any repeating triple-digit. I take that as an invitation to notice what is happening in the moment and say a prayer of gratitude. I also practice seeing magic and miracles in the smallest details of my life. In the twenty years of loading and unloading yoga props from my car almost daily, it has rained on me only a handful of times. I take these small things as signs that I am in the creative vortex and flow of Life. I am where I want to be, and I feel aligned with God and my soul's purpose.

Do you have the radio or television on all the time? Are the voices in your head like a crowded bus station? I invite you to slow down and take a few deep breaths with me. Try to create some quiet in your life. Maybe on your drive home, take a different route and turn off the music, relax your shoulders and focus your attention on your breathing. Just listen. Pay attention to the intuitive hits you get during the day when you just know something without having to think about it. You could also go for a walk and try to look at life around you as if you are seeing it for the very first time. Pay attention to how you feel. I invite you to open your eyes and see what's around you as your day unfolds.

Life speaks to us in many different ways. It might take some practice to notice. So often, our focus is narrow and fixed like we have blinders on. Open your eyes, your ears, and your mind. Expand your field of vision, inside and out. I invite you to approach Life with curiosity, listen with all your senses, hear Life speaking to you, and affirm with me, "Life speaks to me. I listen."

I trust my intuition.

I define intuition as the ability to understand something immediately without the need for conscious reasoning – a kind of "inner knowing." I have learned to listen to and trust my inner knowing because it is usually right.

Whether we call it "empathic," psychic, or "intuitive," this knowing is all about cultivating awareness. Yoga has been a way of cultivating awareness, focusing on meditation, mental clarity, breathing, physical mastery, and spiritual connection. My Toltec training, which came about through reading "The Four Agreements" by Don Miguel Ruiz, was another. I learned how to listen with all my senses to many different streams of information coming to me externally and internally, and to discern which ones to pay attention to. I learned how to stay open and present, and I learned a lot about all the different voices in my head. Some are more helpful than others. It is usually the quiet one under all the noise of the others, the one that comes from my heart, that I trust. I am grateful for all the guidance it gives me, for it is simply the whispering of God in my heart-mind's-eye.

Do you ever just know something without thinking about it? Do you trust it when you do? I invite you to reflect on the times when your intuition has been right, but you dismissed it. For example, sometimes something pops into your head in the grocery store and you discount it, only to find that you are out of that item upon returning home. Listening to and affirming intuition is like strengthening a muscle. The more we listen to intuition and trust it, the stronger it gets and the more we believe it. I invite you to get quiet, take some slow deep breaths and listen. Don't be too quick to brush aside your intuitive prompts. Pay attention to synchronicities and all the ways Life assures us that we are right where we need to be. Join me in affirming, "I trust my intuition."

I love and accept my body.

As I take my teaching to YouTube and put myself in front of the camera, it is sobering to see the weight I have gained in the last couple of years due to aging and injuries. I'm not happy with what I see because I often hold my body up to a false image of perfection, and I tend to judge it as not good enough. I still struggle with this judgment, so I have to return again and again to this affirmation. It helps me turn my judgment around and look past my body's imagined imperfections. I can see my body through the lens of yoga and my commitment to loving myself. Yoga unites body, mind, heart, and spirit into an integrated whole. It is a path to self and to self-love. Yoga, with its focus on compassion, teaches us to love our bodies and ourselves as we are, bellies, warts, and all. I am a 61-year-old man: and, aside from losing a few pounds, I can't change the shape of my body and the fact that I have a belly. After all, Buddha had a belly!

I choose to practice radical self-love today. Having almost lost my life, I accept my body as a miracle of life. My scars and imperfections tell a story, and I am proud of my story. That story is what makes me a real person and not an image of perfection. I choose to focus on Love, and Love doesn't judge. My body is the only one I have this time around, and for that short time, I choose to love it – every pound! At least for today.

The response to my videos has been positive, and that has done wonders for my self-confidence. I am sometimes afraid that you will judge me the way I judge me, but you don't: you see me without those filters, so you love me just the way I am, which helps me to be okay with who I am.

Do you always find something to criticize with your appearance? Are you unhappy with your size and shape, or how you look? Do you avoid looking in mirrors? I invite you to be grateful for the gift of being alive, wherever you are on your healing journey. We all have scars and imperfections, and they tell our stories. I invite you to stop seeing yourself through the filters of your judgment and accept yourself as a miracle of life. Our bodies are precious, and each is a masterpiece of creation that God has gifted to us. So today, I invite you to take a leap, suspend your self-judgment, and join me in affirming, " I love and accept my body."

To speak about self-love, I first have to speak about the anger and self-hatred that grow out of trauma. I was sexually abused as a child and into my teenage years, and that abuse fueled anger, powerlessness, and other feelings I did not know how to process. As a result, I internalized the anger and turned it on myself. I found relief in hurting my body in any way I could, often by overworking to the point of injury, and using alcohol and drugs. I took my anger out on my body even while teaching yoga for many years.

Two decades of Toltec study under teachers in the lineage of Don Miguel Ruiz, author of The Four Agreements, and many trips down to the ancient pyramid city of Teotihuacan, Mexico, have taught me how to see myself, my choices, and my past, through eyes of love and compassion. I broke the agreements that I wasn't good enough and that I was unlovable. I stopped doing things that harmed me and hurt my body.

It has been a long journey of trusting the process of healing and practicing radical self-love. I have nothing but compassion for those younger versions of me that were so angry, in so much pain, and had so few choices. I have found yoga to be the path to self-love that has brought me into a loving relationship with my body. All of these things together have created the life I live and love today.

Do you struggle with self-hatred? This affirmation is a big one. Even if you don't believe it, say it anyway because this affirmation will help you turn your self-hatred into self-love. I believe we all struggle at times with loving ourselves because that's what we do as humans. Next time you look into a mirror, I invite you to see yourself as you would see someone you love, through eyes of love instead of judgment, and have compassion for how hard you work to keep it all together and keep smiling. Getting to this place of self-love can be the journey of a lifetime. Start that journey by affirming with me, "I love myself."

I am a gift to this world.

For a long time, I didn't feel like I was a gift to anyone, much less this world. I didn't love myself and only saw myself through the lens of judgment, not good enough, and self-doubt; how could I possibly be a gift?

Through my recovery and a lot of personal work, I turned that sad story around and learned how to love myself and appreciate the gift of my life. God gave me the gifts of writing, photography, and teaching that I am so grateful for, but I also feel like I have a few other gifts: the gift of my love and compassion, and the big heart I bring to the world. It was a long journey to get to this place of self-love. I hope that the love I feel for myself radiates outward to those around me, and outward from them as well, like ripples on a pond, ever rippling outward. I am a gift to the world just being myself without producing, creating, or doing anything.

I invite us all to see ourselves as gifts to the world. The way you use your words, the twinkle in your eyes, the way you hug and make others laugh, and the way you smile are just a few ways you light up the world by being you. You are also a gift when you are crying, grieving, and afraid. There is strength, power, and healing in being vulnerable with safe people. When we share ourselves authentically, it gives others permission to do the same. I hope you will trust that it's okay to be yourself, and trust that in doing so, you can say with me, "I am a gift to this world."

I shine.

I believe that we each come into this life with our own divine spark or ray of light, a light that is unique to us and singular in the universe. This light is pregnant with possibilities and gifts to share with the world that only we can share. Tragically, our traumas, pain, and suffering can cloud over that spark of light in our hearts; and then on top of that, we build up layers of armor. There were periods in my life when my light was dimmed from depression, illness, and the fog of addiction, but it was still there. Like so many others, I was good at covering my pain with a bright smile and a laugh even when I was suffering on the inside. I was often so judgmental about myself that I couldn't see my own light. Still, people said they could see my light shining through the pain in my eyes. For most of my life, I felt unlovable, not good enough, and unsafe because I didn't know how to love myself or to let love in. I do now.

Since I began my recovery journey over thirty years ago, it has been my life's work to free my heart's light from its armor. I have learned how to clear away the clouds of sadness, addiction, depression, and despair that kept my light from shining outwardly and blocked light and love from coming in. I kept showing up. I wouldn't give up. Every workshop, sweatlodge, retreat, AA meeting, firewalk, and therapy session over those years helped me to understand the layers of armor, how they were making me safe, and how to peel them away one layer at a time. These experiences also gave me the tools to create safety in my life to live the truth of who I authentically am.

One day at a time, one breath at a time, I keep showing up, moving forward, and shining my light. I want the light of my spirit to shine like the sun, and in that shining, I invite you to shine with me. I invite you to open your heart as best as you can and trust that your light is real. Feel the light of your love expressing itself in your shining. Try to see the good in people and challenging situations. Question your judgment, self-hatred, and shame, as these things can block our light. You don't have to strive to shine your light. You can just be who you authentically are: an expression of God's light and love. In our collective shining, we can dispel the clouds of fear, anger, and despair that dim our light these days. I invite you to shine with me. The world needs our light, so affirm with me, "I shine."

The light of God shines through me.

As I understand it, we are all born with a spark of divinity, which I call our vibration. As we clear away the clouds that block that light from shining out and getting in, we raise our vibration. The more we embody love, the higher our vibration, and the higher our vibrations, the more we are in God's frequency and God-consciousness. This allows us to be in the flow of life, to heal, and to manifest our highest intentions. The spark of divinity in us is free to shine.

I am so grateful for the yoga ministry I have been gifted with and the ways I get to be of service and share my light with the world. It is my intention to be a transparent, clear channel of God's light and love. Yoga has been a path to self-love for me, a path to God, and a way of expressing God, which after all is Love. I get to be a mirror for others to see their beauty in. I get to be a channel of light in this world and a channel of God's compassion and love, especially when I teach yoga class. I feel God's words coming out of my mouth, and my movements are guided. The sunlight of God's Love shines out of my eyes, mouth, and heart. My yoga ministry is about more for me than leading the exercises we do on the mat. My ministry is about creating a safe space for God to use my gifts as a healer. At the beginning of every class, I pray to God, "Speak to me. Speak through me".

Many of us are stressed out with the state of our world and might not be feeling much hope or seeing much light in the tragedies that have been happening almost daily. I invite us all to look for the light and the good in others and in life, appreciate it, and own it in ourselves. Our light just is, and it shines whether we intend it or know it. Others can see it, even if we can't. I love the quotation from Les Mis, "To love another person is to see the face of God." We only need to affirm it until we believe it and we know it ourselves.

The eyes are the windows to the soul. Let God's light shine through your eyes, whether you are happy or sad. Jesus said, "Let us be lighthouses among men." We are all lighthouses. I invite you to let others see your light. Trust that it is there even if the clouds of self-doubt get in the way of you seeing it. May we shine our light together and not hide it under a bushel. Join me in affirming, "The light of God shines through me."

Section V : I am Free

Love is the answer.

My heart hurts when I see the hatred, violence, killing, and division we live with daily. How are we going to heal as a nation? How are we going to survive climate change? When will we remove the stigma around mental illness? When will the hate and killing stop?

I know that love is my answer to those questions, because if we were all focused on love, we would not be engaging in violence and conflict. We would be trying to love each other as we are instead of focusing on our differences. People are afraid of what they don't understand; Love opens minds and hearts, and teaches us how to work together instead of against each other.

Before I could bring love to these bigger issues, I had to love myself. As a result of early trauma, I learned to hate myself, and that self-hatred lasted well into my 40s. When I couldn't live up to the image of perfection I held in my mind, I would get angry and judge myself harshly and find some way to punish myself, which usually involved over-work or injury of some kind. It took a lot of hard work to change that. Even though I sometimes struggle with that image of perfection, the self-hatred is gone and I have learned how to bring love to myself. I no longer consciously hurt myself. I know now that I'm good enough and I am lovable.

Whatever your political beliefs, whatever your background, please help me spread love. Each of us can do this, in every moment, in our own little corners of the world -- and that begins with loving ourselves first. I know what it's like to live with self-hatred, and I know what it's like to have that hatred transformed into compassion and love. I have discovered that when we shift our focus from fear to love, healing begins, and love begins to grow in strength and power as we unite together for change.

Love is the answer to so many questions that we face today. How can we love more and fear less? We have to start with ourselves. As the old song said, "let there be peace on earth and let it begin with me." When you look at the world and face the hard questions in your life, I invite you to join me in affirming, "Love is the answer."

I let it go.

We say it a lot, but what does it mean to let something go? I have always been anxious and a worrier. I wish I could have back all the time I spent worrying about things that didn't matter. I know what it's like to have obsessive thoughts, a short attention span, lack of impulse control, and generalized anxiety. I know what it's like to grip and hold tight to something, somebody, or even a belief. I can be pretty rigid at times, micromanaging my life.

Letting something go means to stop giving it my attention. I switch my attention to something else. What I focus my energy on grows. When I am in a state of worry or panic and all I can focus on is the problem, it often escalates and makes the worry and panic bigger, making the solution harder to see. The easiest way I change my thinking is to focus on my breath. Inhale 1,2,3,4. Exhale 1,2,3,4. I repeat this breathing a few more times. I do my best to keep my feet on the ground and give my problems to God. Once I have done that, I trust they will be handled better than I could have on my own. This allows me to live in the moment. When I am successful at changing the channel of my anxiety, worry, or suffering, I feel at peace, empowered, and free. Focusing on gratitude is also a shortcut.

It is not always easy, but it can be done. I do it a lot these days. There are so many things we can let go of; anger, people, situations that cause worry and anxiety, self-harm, labels, resentments, people-pleasing, overdoing, approval seeking, and self-destructive behaviors. I have found the serenity prayer to be helpful as well as the third step prayer from the Big Book of AA. I have created my own version of the prayer (you can find it at the back of the book), and I memorized it so that it could become a part of me. My favorite line reads, "relieve me of the bondage of my fear, judgment, doubt, shame, and guilt, that I be healed, be happy, be whole." We have to find any way we can to put our attention on the solution rather than the problem. The problem or issue may not go away, but we won't be wasting our energy obsessing about it. It is like strengthening a muscle. The more we let go of things that cause us suffering, the more energy can be put into more positive possibilities.

Do you worry too much? Is change hard for you? Do you hold on to anger and resentment? There are so many ways that we hold tight to our beliefs and our opinions. We even hold onto our suffering and pain. Sometimes it's all we know. This holding takes its toll on our bodies and nervous systems, especially anger and resentment. We are living with so much collective stress and tension. In my experience, things usually work out better when we let go of our holding. Let God do for you what you can't do for yourself. I believe in the power of prayer and positive thinking. Give your worry, frustration, and resentment to God. Find your gratitude. Train yourself to change the channel of your attention when you are suffering. Worry is like paying interest on a debt you may never owe. I invite you to join me in affirming, "I let it go."

I can breathe.

I never knew how restricted my breathing was before I began my yoga journey twenty years ago. I have always been anxious, and anxiety constricts my chest, making my breathing shallow. Yoga helped me to recognize this, and yoga taught me how to breathe. Pranayama, or yogic breath practices, taught me to use the breath to balance, relax, ground, and energize. After two decades of practicing yoga, I can finally use my breath to regulate my nervous system when I am feeling anxious and stressed. I have more freedom and expansion with my breath today, which helps immensely with my anxiety and overall health. I have so much less anxiety than I used to.

Of course, we breathe all the time, but do we breathe consciously with all of our lung capacity? When was the last time you took a full, relaxed breath from your belly to your collar bones? The deeper we breathe, the more oxygen we inhale, and more oxygen means clearer thinking, more energy, and better mental and physical health. It's a matter of expansion and contraction. When we are anxious, angry, and afraid, we contract, and our breathing becomes restricted and shallow. When we are relaxed and at peace we are in a state of expansion, which puts the whole body into rest and digest mode, which boosts the immune system and facilitates healing.

To inspire means to take a breath. When we are inspired by something, it means we are taking it in as we would a breath. When I say this affirmation, I feel a freedom from tension and contraction I never felt before. I feel more open to inspiration, more relaxed, and expansive. It also brings me into my body. I feel grounded. My inhale puts me in touch with goodness and light and positivity, and exhaling lets me release heaviness and tension. One deep breath can change my thoughts and emotions and open me to new possibilities. Putting all my attention on my breath, my mind has stopped racing ahead and judging the last word that came out of my mouth or into my thoughts. I take a few more breaths and notice a real shift in the way I feel. I take a few minutes to slow down, pause, and breathe mindfully. I invite you to notice all the things that you feel when you join me in affirming, "I can breathe."

I invite you to take a few minutes to join me in a guided breathing meditation on gratitude. You might close your eyes at the end of each paragraph to go inside a little more deeply, or you could keep them open if that feels right for you.

Notice your breath as it comes in and out of your mouth and nose – just notice it, and take a couple of deeper breaths in and out of your nose, or in your nose and out your mouth. Notice where you are, what you are sitting or lying on, and feel how it supports you. Feel the ground under your feet. Feel your clothing on your skin, noticing where it feels tight or loose. Feel the air on your exposed skin.

Now, start to breathe in to the count of four and out to the count of four. As you slow down, notice the pause between your inhale and your exhale, and your exhale and your inhale. Follow your breath as it enters your nostrils and moves around in the back of your throat; follow it down into your lungs, filling up your belly first, then your lower chest and upper chest. Your lungs go all the way up to the collar bones, so you might feel it all the way up there. You might also feel your lungs expand like a pair of balloons in every direction. Don't push your breath; breathe as it feels good and natural.

Now try to slow your breathing down a bit more, putting your awareness in your neck and shoulders on your inhale. Notice any tension there. Soften and relax your neck and shoulders on your exhale, parting your teeth and relaxing your mouth, jaw, and tongue. Notice the tension beginning to ease and melt away.

I invite you to think of something or someone you are grateful for, just breathing into your appreciation. Continue to be mindful of your breathing as your heart opens up with appreciation for everything you are grateful for. When your mind wanders – and it will! – continue to bring your awareness back to gratitude and to your breath, as you focus your mind on the simple inhale and exhale of breath.

You have stepped into the present moment. The present moment is, after all, where life is happening. Take a moment and notice how you feel. In just this short time you have connected to your heart and your breath. Your breath is always there and it is always a gift. Say thank you to yourself for taking a moment to connect with yourself and slow down. Let us inhale positive thoughts of intention and exhale any resistance to them. Join me in affirming, "My breath connects me to the present moment."

My Center is a still pond.

I have been anxious and hyper-vigilant all my life, and I have struggled to manage and regulate an overactive nervous system. Medication helps and I am grateful for it, but the biggest help has been the gift of peace from my yoga and meditation practice. I am using all my yoga tools these days, and some days it's more difficult to find peace than others. Sometimes, the pressure of the challenges we are facing now in our world is more than I am able to process.

On days like that, it requires the discipline of spiritual practice. I understand spiritual discipline as being a disciple to my higher self. It is anything I do with intention that will connect me with God, Source, Spirit, and my own higher self. This includes studying myself, caring for myself, and doing everything for the benefit of my higher self. As we say in AA, "to thine own self be true." It takes real training in a dedicated manner to build good habits, especially a meditation practice. My feeling of connection started small, but it has gotten bigger over time as I was able to sit with myself more easily for longer amounts of time.

The care of my nervous system also requires lots of peace and quiet. I have four water fountains in my house, so there is always the soothing sound of water. I have created a sanctuary in my home with many beautiful plants. The discipline of my spiritual practice has created a safe space around me and deep inside of me that is untouched by what's going on in the world, filled with healing energy for my anxiety and ravaged nervous system.

We have this amazing gift of our imagination, which we can use as a tool to step out of our suffering and go into our heart space, where our love, compassion, understanding, and gratitude live. This has a powerful effect on our nervous system, bringing us back into equilibrium. For example, we can visualize ourselves in Nature at a beautiful pond. Cattails surround it. Lily pads float on it. Dragonflies and butterflies buzz around the red, pink, and yellow water lilies. There is birdsong in the fresh, clean air, and white puffy clouds drift lazily across a turquoise sky.

Connecting with this place requires us to take a few moments to stop, close our eyes, and breathe, to help us get grounded and centered. It gives us a safe place deep inside of us where we can go when we find ourselves rushing around needlessly and feeling stressed.

I find it helpful to take a few moments out of each day to stop and do this practice, to this place when I need it. I invite you to try it when you are off center and spend as long as you like in your peaceful place. What can you imagine that will take you into this healing place deep inside you, calm your heart and mind, and bring you peace? I invite you to join me in affirming, "My center is a still pond."

I am content.

One of the niyamas in yoga is santosha, which is defined as "complete contentment." The niyamas are inner observances for how we relate to ourselves. For example, I have a short attention span, and I used to rush around wanting to be somewhere other than where I was, not comfortable in my skin. My striving for perfection in the form of approval-seeking and people-pleasing kept me far from content. I couldn't sit still long enough to take a breath, much less be content. It has taken years to cultivate the niyama of "complete contentment" and relax into the present moment.

My journey to contentment came from self-love, which grew out of sobriety, self-study, yoga, meditation, and hard work. I still have moments where I rush around anxiously, but the overarching feeling in my life is contentment. I try to do things I enjoy with people I love and enjoy, so I don't want to be anywhere other than where I am. It is a choice to slow down and to stop wanting the next shiny thing that catches my eye. We are bombarded with messages day and night that if we just did or had X, Y, or Z, we would be happy, good enough, or loveable. I am learning to stop comparing my body and my life to those of other people.

I am grateful for the simple and quiet life I have created. It slows me down and nourishes me greatly. Teddy is a wonderful partner and provides a safe haven where I can continue to heal. We snuggle and hold hands whenever we can, at the movies, riding in the car, and sitting in front of the TV. I have created a sanctuary in my home filled with plants, water fountains, and light. I spend a lot of time in silence. I enjoy my own company. I laugh a lot and I live with so much less anxiety than I used to. The work I do with my yoga ministry nourishes my soul, and my two cats, Kim and Lily, delight me endlessly and take good care of me with their pussycat ways.

Do you rush around 'multi-tasking,' constantly distracted? Do you have a short attention span? Do you enjoy your own company? I invite you to explore when, where, and how you already feel content. Practicing gratitude and self-love got me to this place of contentment. I invite you to find what relaxes you. Explore what contentment means to you and what you might do to increase it in your life. Stop trying so hard and know that your best is good enough. I have learned that happiness is an inside job. I invite you to slow down with me and take a breath. Join me in affirming, "I am content."

I am at peace.

The end of this book has found me. It has been three years since I posted my first affirmation meme on Facebook. I had no idea at the time that three years later I would be here realizing the dream of writing a book. You have learned a lot about me: where my pain came from, what I did with it, and how I healed it. I have made myself vulnerable and have at times laid fetal on the bed with anxiety about sharing such personal details about my life. I am a teacher with a wall of degrees in the challenges of being a gay man in a sometimes harsh and unforgiving world. I grew up in an affluent family, and I have done things and seen parts of the world that many could only dream of, but there was also a price. The price was trauma, and it is a miracle that I survived until 60.

After decades of Toltec work, healing, recovery, and devoted yoga practice, I am at peace in my life. Yoga gave me meditation, and The Toltec path helped me cultivate awareness, love, and transformation with the power of my intention. I have been in recovery for half of my life. I said yes to help, yes to God, and yes to Life. I am proud of the man I am and the hard-earned wisdom I have. My recovery from codependency has been nothing less than miraculous: I no longer let others make decisions for me, and my happiness no longer depends on the happiness of others. I create less drama and experience fewer extreme mountains and valleys. I spend a lot of time quietly in my home, my sanctuary and safety zone. An 11-year relationship with my partner Teddy has grown me and nourished me in so many different ways and on so many different levels.

I hope that I have fought all my battles and climbed all my mountains, but regardless, I will continue to move forward one step at a time, one day at a time, trusting Life to support me. I try to be a beacon of love in the world. I try to live with integrity and authenticity. I want to be transparent as a teacher and an example of what a recovery path might look like, even if it's a bit out of the box. I try not to have regrets, and I try to be a good partner, brother, uncle, and friend. It is my hope this book will inspire self-love and give support in the process of healing to someone who is suffering. Thank you for sharing this affirmation journey with me. I hope it has been helpful. Take a breath and join me in affirming this last affirmation; "I am at peace."

Afterword : We are Artists. Our Lives are our Art

As I look out over all of my affirmation memes spread out on the floor in preparation for publishing, I see a beautiful patchwork of color. I have put so much of my story of healing and my triumph over many challenges into these affirmation memes. In doing so, I have opened up my heart and made myself more transparent and vulnerable. I have shared truths and stories of hard work and healing. As I look over the memes, I see that my life is made of millions and millions of little choices, each choice like a stroke of paint on a canvas or a note of a song. There are so many different colors, layers, shapes, and textures of Life. It may not be a Rembrandt or a Picasso, but it is rich with so much beauty because it is mine, and what I have painted is unique to me and unlike anyone else's.

Because it is my work of art, I can paint over parts that no longer represent who I am or start over with a blank canvas anytime I want to. I've had to do that many times. As I learn from my mistakes and grow, my skill and my art evolve. There were times when I was happy and painted with all the colors of the rainbow. There were times when I was ill or depressed when there was no color at all. Today I choose carefully and mindfully as I create my life with skill, awareness, integrity, curiosity, gratitude, unconditional love, and authenticity. Maybe the last thing you would call your life is "art," but I say it is. The challenge is to appreciate your artistic expression without judgments or comparisons. We spend way too much time judging ourselves and comparing ourselves to others, when most people are self-absorbed enough that they are not giving us that much attention. Think about every choice you make in a day and think about how many are unconscious and habitual. What would it be like to imagine you could paint your life by consciously choosing how you want it? I believe we create our reality with our thoughts and actions, and what we focus our attention on grows. As you finish your first time reading this book, know that this is an ongoing process for me, and I invite you to use it in your own ongoing journey. You can open it at random each day and use the affirmation in front of you as your meditation for the day. Use these as a jumping-off point to create your own affirmations! There are so many things we can affirm as we walk our unique path of healing.

I also invite you to be curious and to change some of the little choices that are unconscious and habitual. Think about what you could bring into your life to make you happier. Changing a belief system starts with changing just one thought. Surround yourself with things and people that bring you joy and express your soul. Find who and what inspires you. Life doesn't have to be so serious. It's okay if it's not perfect. It's not meant to be. Life is messy sometimes, and that is art too. Sing, write, dance or play your next note, word, step, or game. I invite you to be conscious of your choices and take some risks. Look at yourself and your life through the eyes of love and compassion. Say "Yes" to your own life.

Resources : Prayer and Meditations

My Third Step Prayer

When I joined Alcoholics Anonymous, I was encouraged to memorize the Third Step Prayer. In the beginning, I said it as it was written and I said it often. I loved the prayer so much that I started adapting it for myself from a trauma-recovery point of view. I said this prayer almost hourly when I was in difficult situations or making transitions in my life. For example, 2013 was a huge year of change for me as I closed down the community of Laughing Winds and scattered its inhabitants to the four directions, and moved to Clarksville to be closer to my partner Teddy. It was the biggest act of power in my codependency recovery, but it took me over a year to get over it. This prayer gave me the strength to make it through the challenge of setting myself free.

I still say this prayer before I teach a yoga class or when the digits line up on the clock - 1:11, 2:22, 3:33, etc. It's a powerful prayer, and it is probably the biggest gift from AA that I still use on a daily, sometimes hourly basis.

Mother/Father God, I offer myself to you. To build with, create with, and heal with me, as you will it.

Relieve me from the bondage of my fear, judgment, self-hatred, doubt, guilt and shame, so that I may be healed, be happy, be whole.

Take away these difficulties, that my light will shine in this world, and that I would be a witness to those I would help: of your power, your love, and your way of life.

May I do your will always.

May my open heart be a channel for your compassion, love, and grace.

May I feel safe, and trust the process of healing.

May I know how very much I am loved!

Adapted from the third step prayer from Alcoholics Anonymous
- David W Jones

Meditation: This Too Shall Pass

Find a quiet place where you won't be disturbed for 10 minutes or so. You might sit in a chair or lie on a bed or the floor, whatever is most comfortable. Start by taking some deep breaths. Breathe in to the count of four, and out to the count of four, pausing between the inhale and the exhale, and then between the exhale and the inhale. Part your teeth and relax your jaw. Soften any tension and holding in your shoulders, neck, and face. Sense your breath as it enters through your nostrils. Feel it moving around in the back of your throat. Follow it as it flows down into the bottom of your lungs filling up your belly, then your middle chest, then up into the top of your lungs. Breathe from your belly all the way up to your collarbones.

I invite you to think of a difficult time in your life. Perhaps a serious illness or something you did not think you were going to get through, or a situation you couldn't see your way out of. Remember how the fear felt in your body. Now see how the situation or problem was resolved and feel the shift in your body. Whether the outcome was good or bad, it eventually passed, and it is now a distant memory. Everything you have ever dreaded has passed. Notice how this insight feels in your body, too.

Time passes and our point of view changes as our feelings change. Everything in this Universe is in constant motion. What is stressing you today probably won't matter in a year, two, or five.

Now see yourself sitting on the bank of a river. Notice how you feel just sitting by the flowing river, watching a leaf and a twig float by. It's a beautiful day. The sun is warm on your skin and you feel a light breeze. You feel the earth under you.

Now, see yourself safe in an inner-tube floating lazily down the river. The current is slow and gentle. How does it feel to leave the bank behind and trust that the river will carry you to where you need to be? To prosperity, opportunity, and blessing?

Breathe in the sounds of insects and birds and feel what it feels like to float down the river. A dragonfly comes to rest on your knee. Watch the iridescent light play on its gossamer wings.

Let yourself be in a place of safety and trust, letting your whole body relax. Look up at the blue sky and watch the white, puffy clouds slowly pass by, letting all your cares and worries pass by with the scenery as you float down the river. Feel how good it is to be alive. Take a couple more deep breaths into that feeling and slowly open your eyes.

The river is a metaphor for your life. Is it your habit to grasp at the roots and reeds on the bank, trying to stay where you are? Or even to swim against the current, trying to resist the flow of the river, always over-working and pushing yourself hard to get where you think you have to be?

It's scary to let go of control, but it is also freeing and it opens us up to new possibilities. Try not to get too attached to what is stressing you out and causing you suffering right now. See yourself in the flow of Life, happy, confident, and in a place of trust. I invite you to tell yourself, "This too shall pass. It always passes."

Namaste~

Meditation: On Gratitude

Find a quiet place where you won't be disturbed for 10 minutes or so. You might sit in a chair or lie on a bed or the floor, whatever is most comfortable. Start by taking some deep breaths. Breathe in to the count of four, and out to the count of four, pausing between the inhale and the exhale, and then between the exhale and the inhale. Part your teeth and relax your jaw. Soften any tension and holding in your shoulders, neck, and face. Sense your breath as it enters through your nostrils. Feel it moving around in the back of your throat. Follow it as it flows down into the bottom of your lungs filling up your belly, then your middle chest, then up into the top of your lungs. Breathe from your belly all the way up to your collarbones.

I invite you to think of someone you are grateful for. Think of what you love about this person and feel all your appreciation for them. Let the feeling of gratitude fill you. If it feels good, allow another person to come to mind and experience your gratitude for them. Take as long as you need, letting people come before your heart-mind's eye, and feel your appreciation for each one of them. Feel how your gratitude grows for each person. Now, take a moment to think of a life lesson you learned the hard way. As you reflect on that experience, remember everything – inside and out – that got you through, and the lessons you learned in the process. Bring to mind your gratitude for those who helped you during that time. Maybe even say thank you to them. Feel your gratitude for getting through that difficult time.

Now, think of all the experiences that are easy to be grateful for. Bring image after image of things and experiences you are grateful for into your heart-mind's eye. Let each experience fill your heart with appreciation. Gratitude uplifts our spirits and feeds our hearts. Continue breathing slowly and deeply and notice how this gratitude meditation has brought you into the present moment; present with your breath, present with your heart, present with your love and appreciation.

Before you rise up from the meditation, be sure to thank yourself for taking a few minutes out of your day to stop and simply be present with your gratitude. Notice how you feel. Do you feel different? There is always something to be grateful for.

Namaste~

Meditation: On Forgiveness

Find a quiet place where you won't be disturbed for 10 minutes or so. You might sit in a chair or lie on a bed or the floor, whatever is most comfortable. Start by taking some relaxing deep breaths. Breathe in to the count of four, and out to the count of four, pause between the inhale and the exhale, and then between the exhale and the inhale. Part your teeth and relax your jaw. Soften any tension and holding in your shoulders, neck, and face. Sense your breath as it enters through your nostrils. Feel it moving around in the back of your throat. Follow it as it flows down into the bottom of your lungs filling up your belly, then your middle chest, then up into the top of your lungs. Breathe from your belly all the way up to your collarbones.

I invite you to join me on a journey of the heart. See yourself in a forest of giant redwoods. There are soft needles on the ground and the tall trees make it seem like you are in a cathedral. It is quiet. Feel the air on your skin. It's a beautiful day. There is birdsong, but the atmosphere is quiet and holy.

You are walking on the soft ground when you hear the sound of water. You follow the sound until you come to a waterfall. The beauty of it takes your breath away. It's exhilarating and relaxing at the same time.

I invite you to sit comfortably on the water's edge. There is beauty all around you. Breathe it in. The sound and smells, the power of the falling water. You are being held in the unconditional love of Nature. Your thoughts get lost in the falling water as your heart begins to open and soften.

I invite you to reflect on some of the lies you have told others and those you told mostly to yourself. Think about some of the times you held yourself up to a false image of perfection, and the approval-seeking that went with that. Think about your addictions and the wreckage you caused because of them. Reflect on all the times you've hated yourself and the judgments and punishments you've inflicted on yourself.

Witness everything that comes up without judgment and notice how you feel. I invite you to recognize that you were only trying to medicate your pain. Breathe into your heart, let it soften around everything you're feeling, and have compassion for yourself; you have always done your best with what you have had to work with. Take yourself off the hook and set yourself free.

Imagine that your self-hatred, shame, and judgment are like a heavy coating of mud, that you have lived with all your life. Now see yourself stepping into that waterfall as you would step into a shower, and let the falling water wash it all away. Feel the exhilaration and lightness of the water washing you clean.

Forgiveness is an act of self-love. Wrap your arms around your torso and tell yourself "I forgive you. I love you." Enjoy how it feels to simply hold yourself and feel love radiating throughout your body.

Thank yourself for taking time out of your day to do this healing meditation and connect to your heart. Forgiveness is freedom. Focus on your breath and your gratitude.

Slowly open your eyes and come back to the room you are in and the sounds and sights around you. Notice how you feel. You do not have to carry the burden of your guilt and shame on your shoulders or in your heart anymore. Breathe into this feeling of freedom. It is only a breath away.

Namaste~

Meditation: For Self-Love

Find a quiet place where you won't be disturbed for 10 minutes or so. You might sit in a chair or lie on a bed or the floor, whatever is most comfortable. Start by taking some deep breaths. Breathe in to the count of four, and out to the count of four, pausing between the inhale and the exhale, and then between the exhale and the inhale. Part your teeth and relax your jaw. Soften any tension and holding in your shoulders, neck, and face. Sense your breath as it enters through your nostrils. Feel it moving around in the back of your throat. Follow it as it flows down into the bottom of your lungs filling up your belly, then your middle chest, then up into the top of your lungs. Breathe from your belly all the way up to your collarbones.

I invite you to think of some of the people who love you, and who you love; perhaps partners, siblings, grandparents, or your best friends. See them smiling at you and let yourself take in their love. Take a mental picture of them looking at you, as they tell you they love you.

Now, imagine there is a white wall behind your closed eyelids, and imagine putting all the pictures of these people on the wall in front of you. Bathe in the love that washes over you as you look at each image. Now take in the whole wall, feeling all the love these people hold for you. Take a few minutes with this! Open your heart to the love radiating from them to you and breathe in that love. Feel it filling you up inside. This love is yours, and you can use it to love yourself. If they love you, you can love you, and that love becomes your own.

As you feel that love in your heart, see yourself as a young child. Any age that feels right is fine. Notice how you feel seeing a younger version of yourself. Notice how they feel. Are they happy or sad? What does it feel like to look at them with love? What would you tell this child if you could talk to them? How might you comfort this child or make them feel at ease? How could you share the love in your heart with them? Ask this younger version of yourself if you could give them a hug. Feel your open-hearted connection with this child. Breathe it in.

Now we are going to focus on feeling this love in your body. Put your left hand over your heart. Feel it beating. Feel the power of every beat. I invite you to picture a bright diamond in your heart center, with light shining out of every facet, glowing from within. Its light is your love radiating outwards. Put your right hand over your left and feel the power of the love you are feeling. Be present to the rise and fall of your belly and chest as you breathe.

I invite you to tell yourself, "I love you." It doesn't matter if you believe it; try saying it anyway – that's what affirmations are for! Wrap your arms around your torso and feel the strength of your arms holding you. Rest in this feeling as long as you like.

Now take a few slow breaths as you begin to open your eyes and come back to the world around you. Notice how you feel. Thank yourself for taking these few minutes to connect with your own love.

Namaste~

Meditation: My Center is a Still Pond

Find a quiet place where you won't be disturbed for 10 minutes or so. You might sit in a chair or lie on a bed or the floor, whatever is most comfortable. Start by taking some relaxing deep breaths. Breathe in to the count of four, and out to the count of four, pause between the inhale and the exhale, and then between the exhale and the inhale. Part your teeth and relax your jaw. Soften any tension and holding in your shoulders, neck, and face. Sense your breath as it enters through your nostrils. Feel it moving around in the back of your throat. Follow it as it flows down into the bottom of your lungs filling up your belly, then your middle chest, then up into the top of your lungs. Breathe from your belly all the way up to your collarbones.

I invite you to close your eyes with me and visualize deep inside of you a place that is unaffected by things going on outside of you. I see this place as being a still pond surrounded by reeds and cattails. Beautiful pink and white water lilies float on the pond as dragonflies and butterflies buzz about them. The surface reflects a turquoise blue sky with puffy white clouds lazily passing by. The sounds of insects and birdsong make the air you are breathing come to life.

There is a light breeze, and you feel the sun's warmth on your skin. It's a perfect day. Take as much time as you like to lie on the grass and feel the earth under your body. Look up at the sky, letting the tension in your neck and shoulders melt away as you feel the earth supporting you. I invite you to breathe into this calm, quiet place. Soften any remaining tension in your jaw and shoulders, think of all that you are grateful for, and feel the love that resonates in your heart when you let go of judgments and doubts, and let your heart open. Take a mental picture of all that you see so you can find your way here again. I invite you to feel the deep peace of connecting with Nature and your heart. Stay here as long as you wish.

Slowly begin to open your eyes and bring yourself back to your surroundings and the sounds around you. I invite you to take a few more slow relaxed breaths before you get up and go about your day. Be with this peaceful feeling as long as you can. Keep that mental picture inside of you alive. Make it your own. Your place of safety and stillness might be different from mine. You can be confident that there is a peaceful place deep inside of you that is only a breath and a visualization away.

Namaste~

Photo Credits

Cover: Teddy Jones
Section 1: David W Jones
1   David W. Jones
2   Teddy Jones
3   Jeff Johnston
4   David W Jones
5   David W Jones
6   Tom Clephane
7   Alice Ann White Schlemm
8   Meditation
9   Hunter Flournoy
10 Alice Ann White Schlemm
11 David W Jones

Section 2: Teddy Jones
1   David W Jones
2   David W Jones
3   David W Jones
4   Teddy Jones
5   David W. Jones
6   David W Jones
7   Harry Pemberton
8   Teddy Jones
9   Tish & Dave Kashdan
10 Teddy Jones

Section 3: Teddy Jones
1   David W Jones
2   David W Jones
3   David W Jones
4   David W Jones
5   David W Jones
6   Teddy Jones
7   Alice Ann White Schlemm
8   Susan Kolb
9   David W Jones
10 David W Jones
11 David W Jones
12 David W Jones

Section IV: Teddy Jones
1   David W Jones
2   David W Jones
3   Ben Kashdan
4   Teddy Jones
5   David W Jones
6   Teddy Jones
7   Teddy Jones
8   Suzy Hopkins
9   David W Jones
10 David W Jones

Section V: David W Jones
1   David W Jones
2   David W Jones
3   David W Jones
4   David W Jones
5   Alice Ann White Schlemm
6   David W Jones
7   David W Jones
8   David W Jones

Afterword: Teddy Jones
                    David W Jones
Resources: David W Jones
My prayer: David W Jones

CPSIA information can be obtained
at www.ICGtesting.com
Printed in the USA
LVHW071630011222
733834LV00001BA/1